HORIZON

SPRING, 1975 • VOLUME XVII, NUMBER 2

cHorizon

SPRING, 1975 · VOLUME XVII, NUMBER 2

HORIZON is published every three months by American Heritage Publishing Co., Inc. Editorial and executive offices: 1221 Avenue of the Americas, New York, N.Y. 10020. Treasurer: Marjorie C. Dyer. Secretary: William Cusick. All correspondence about subscriptions should be addressed to: HORIZON Subscription Office, 379 West Center St., Marion, Ohio 43302.

Single copies: $7.50. Subscriptions: $26.00 per year in the U.S.; Canada and elsewhere. $28.00.

Cumulative indexes for Volumes I–V, VI–X, and XI–XV are available at $5. HORIZON is also indexed in the *Readers' Guide to Periodical Literature.* The editors welcome contributions but can assume no responsibility for unsolicited material. Title registered U.S. Patent Office. Second-class postage paid at New York, N.Y., and at additional mailing offices.

Out of Africa—and Milton, Del.

Isak Dinesen

One of the real pleasures of editing a magazine is that mail sometimes comes in from the readers. These letters are often full of praise and information and, once in a while, indignation. But now and then a communication arrives that is particularly gratifying and illuminating, as, for example, when a subscriber from Milton, Delaware, recently informed us that HORIZON "lifts the burden of the suffering around us—whether, in our personal lives, or in far-off Israel, Vietnam, Cyprus, or drought-ridden Africa." By this he meant, we take it, not that we merely offer an easy escape from current miseries but that we try to make whatever sense of them we can: to think about what humanity has achieved and whether it is worth preserving.

Surely the hardest-won achievement in history has been a decent system of government. The republic is an ancient invention, but in the long run republics have not had a high survival rate. In this issue of HORIZON, three of our regular contributors, J.H. Plumb, (on inflation, page 46), Edmond Taylor (on secret agents, page 4), and Walter Karp (on the death of republics, page 14), point out that our own republic may have been exposed to certain dangerous diseases. Perhaps we can avoid catching them, or at least manage not to die of them. But we should not, our authors imply, make the mistake of assuming that democracies are immortal. Governments do change, and not always for the better, and countries do sometimes vanish from the map.

Beginning on page 102, as it happens, is a poignant look at one such country—British East Africa, where Isak Dinesen went to live in 1913 and which she recreated so beguilingly in her classic memoir, *Out of Africa.* The photographs we present come from her family album, and they provide a moving glimpse into a world that is lost. In those days Isak Dinesen was Baroness Karen Blixen, the young Danish wife of a

Swedish planter who had settled near Nairobi. They were eventually to be divorced, and the baroness ran the coffee plantation herself until 1931, when she was forced to depart, bankrupt. Returning to Denmark and a writing career, she had her first success in 1934 with *Seven Gothic Tales. Out of Africa* followed, in 1938 and made her quite deservedly famous. But it is one of those books that time has altered. Vivid and delectable as it is, in 1975 it has a strange ring to it.

British East Africa, as she describes it, is, of course, a colony farmed by Europeans under whose direction labor "the Natives," mostly Kikuyu tribesmen. The baroness, imaginative and humane, managed her staff quite well. "It was not easy to get to know the Natives," she writes. "They were quick of hearing and evanescent; if you frightened them, they could withdraw into a world of their own, in a second, like the wild animals which at an abrupt movement from you are gone,—simply are not there." She depicts herself among these gazelle-like creatures, assessing their virtues and faults ("The Natives, who have a strong sense of rhythm, know nothing of verse . . ."), complaining gently of their fecklessness. The picture she draws of them is so enchanting, in fact, that it is an effort to recall what was next to occur in the colony.

For, of course, it was these same Kikuyu from whom the Mau Mau arose in the 1950's to slaughter the landowners. Jomo Kenyatta was working for the water department in Nairobi while Baroness Blixen was growing coffee nearby; he had been educated at the Church of Scotland Mission, which she sometimes visited. Did they brush against each other in the streets? Did she pause to compare him with the antelope? In 1963, the year after her death, Kenyatta became the first prime minister of the nation of Kenya. He still rules. Among Kenya's present problems are malnutrition and the looming possibility of famine, and an exceptionally high birth rate. So we're back again to current miseries.

The world that Isak Dinesen inhabited is gone, and we are fortunate to have a few pictures of it. Feudal societies always have a romantic tug, especially for those who have never had to live in one. We are fortunate also to have her book about British East Africa— a true pastoral, it has been called. Aside from its other merits, it is documentation of a change in human attitudes. The colonial mentality is headed for extinction. We have our own brand of racism in the 1970's, but at least any talk about "the Natives" is likely to be taken as a joke. —S.T.

THE PIERPONT MORGAN LIBRARY, M.736

COVER: These seagoing cockleshells are Viking ships —or at least were intended as such by the twelfth-century English artist who painted them. The miniature comes from a manuscript called "The Miracles of St. Edmund," which includes a description of the Viking invasion of England in the ninth century, and an enumeration of their wartime atrocities. An article about these rough customers begins on page 64. Among the illustrations accompanying it are other miniatures from the same manuscript.

THE CULT OF
THE SECRET AGENT

In fact as in fiction the spy
is the indispensable man of our time.
Yet his activity poses
a deadly threat to the open society

From the standpoint of the historian, the man who touched off the greatest political scandal in our entire national existence—the former CIA officer, ex-White House consultant, and convicted Watergate conspirator E. Howard Hunt—has by now dwindled to a relatively secondary figure in the drama. Hunt's career as a secret agent by day and a writer of spy-and-sex novels by night, his picturesque extracurricular capers, his delusive right-wing mythology—all these seem no more than material for a colorful footnote. Thus, in *The Imperial Presidency*, Arthur M. Schlesinger, Jr., allots almost as much space to the "forgotten hero," Frank Wills, the security guard in the Watergate complex whose vigilance may have saved the republic (we all have to assume it has been saved), as he does to the imperial plumber whose bungling was no less crucial to exposing the conspiracy. (It was Hunt's name, found in the address book of one of the arrested Watergate burglars operating under him, that led investigators to the door of the White House.) "I had known Howie Hunt since we worked together in the first days of the Marshall Plan in Paris in 1948," Professor Schlesinger recalls. "He was an amiable writer of cheap thrillers, a *fantaisiste* now suddenly empowered by a President of the United States to live out his fantasies."

The conspiratorial dream world Hunt lived in was clearly built on his identification with the romanticized and idealized image of the secret agent, one of the most characteristic projections of twentieth-century mass culture. This glamorous figure has served as the hero of countless films, plays, comic strips, pulp magazine stories, and novels, including the forty-odd written by Hunt himself under various pen names. James Bond, the steel-thewed sexual athlete, jet-set brand-name dropper, and bureaucratized killer invented by the late Ian Fleming (himself a World War II British intelligence officer), is probably the most famous of these synthetic modern heroes, but Hunt's fictional *Doppelgänger,* Peter Ward, an ace CIA operative with a special, not to say compulsive, gift for conducting flawless "entry operations," is equally illustrative—and in certain respects, one fears, more authentic.

Fictional depictions of the secret agent as hero are validated in the public mind by an almost equally abundant flow of nonfictional accounts—in memoirs, biographies, histories, studies, exposés—of real intelligence operations and real secret agents. (It is amazing how loquacious a supposedly sealed-lips profession can be.) Much of this material, even when technically factual, is hardly less mythologized in its presentation than the purely imaginary adventures of a James Bond or a Peter Ward. Some real-life heroes of the secret service world, while remaining within hailing distance of historical truth, have shown themselves to be masters of self-romanticization. T. E. Lawrence is the supreme example, but others—like Richard Sorge, the World War II Soviet secret agent in Japan who scored, albeit to no avail, one of the great intelligence scoops of modern times, or Sidney Reilly, a British undercover operator in early postrevolutionary Russia who was possibly the most audacious, and probably the most unpleasant, spy of any time—have accomplished feats that stimulated the journalistic or novelistic imagination and at the same time enhanced their credibility. Still others have captured the public imagination because their stories sounded like something out of a book—usually a pretty bad one.

In all secret service literature, fiction and nonfiction alike, there is an ambiguous and extremely complex relationship

By EDMOND TAYLOR

WITH A PAINTING FOR HORIZON BY DENNIS CORRIGAN

between myth and reality. Such a relationship exists, indeed, within the covert organizations themselves. Somerset Maugham, who served in the British Secret Intelligence Service during World War I, was probably the first modern writer to be struck by the tendency of the secret service to imitate art—the art of the popular thriller. This phenomenon, which might be termed the Ashenden Effect after the eponymous hero of Maugham's semiautobiographical espionage tales, has since been confirmed by a number of other writers of secret service fiction—most notably Graham Greene and Compton Mackenzie—who have themselves had actual secret service experience. (I noticed the same tendency myself—and at moments in myself—during my five years' service in General William J. Donovan's Office of Strategic Services in World War II.)

Thus the writer of spy thrillers or romanticized secret service history and the real-life covert operator are dialectical partners. The former, by glamorizing the secret agent, creates an archetype upon which the latter tends to model his professional behavior, and he in turn authenticates the writer's fantasy. This dialectic goes a long way toward explaining the hold the secret agent has acquired on the popular imagination.

For the secret agent is more than a mere collective fantasy exploited for entertainment, like such comparable, if dated, synthetic folk heroes as the cowboy, the great detective, and the gangbuster. Entertainment is only his cover. Though it is hard to write about him, or even think about him, without mentally putting one's tongue in one's cheek, he is not really a figure of fun. More and more he appears to be assuming the role of a culture hero in the true sense: a mythical personification of the aspirations and ideals of a society, or, if not a whole society, a dangerously large segment of one—specifically ours. Perhaps even more disquieting, as the hero's mythical stature grows, the moral values he incarnates seem to degenerate. James Bond is a more sinister figure than the gentlemanly amateur agents with whom

John Buchan's readers identified, and Howard Hunt's Peter Ward is in several respects still worse. His typically professional moral nihilism, unlike Bond's, is overlaid with a kind of paranoid self-righteousness. He voices it toward the end of one of his nastier adventures (*On Hazardous Duty*, the story of how Ward blackmails a Soviet agent into defecting). In an eerily prescient reflection, he says, "We become lawless in the struggle for the rule of the law."

To Americans, the most dramatic illustration of what might be called the Peter Ward Syndrome—the tendency to base one's world outlook and moral attitudes upon those of the imaginary secret agent—has been furnished by the Watergate scandals. The trend is not, however, peculiar to the United States. On the contrary, it appears to be worldwide—though there are hopeful signs of a countertrend here and there— and its most explicit manifestations are seen in Soviet Russia and its European satellites.

That the secret service and secret police mentalities permeate the party-state power apparatus of the Soviet Union and its Warsaw Pact allies is hardly news. Up to a few years ago, however, the Communist secret agent— whether spy, "black" propaganda specialist, covert political subversionist, or some other clandestine operator—was not a Soviet culture hero, or even a familiar figure on the Soviet cultural scene. The revolutionary agitator, the wartime guerrilla, at moments the internal security or counterespionage officer —they might be heroes, but not the undercover agent, operating against foreign targets generally outside the party framework. Though the foiling of "imperialist" and especially American plots against the Socialist Fatherland was a popular theatrical and cinematic theme during the 1950's, the spy thriller, like its cousin the detective story, was still regarded by the custodians of Soviet culture as a mind-drugging by-product of bourgeois decadence.

As Sanche de Gramont noted in his book *The Secret War*, Soviet policy toward spy stories began to change after 1961, when the country's novelists, playwrights, and scenarists were chided by a congress of writers in Moscow for failing to dramatize the heroism of Soviet underground agents abroad and the importance of their services to the nation. Since then, the flowering of spy stories and films in the U.S.S.R. has become so exuberant as to inspire satirical cartoons in the Soviet literary press. In Bulgaria one writer created a homegrown Marxist analogue of James Bond, an invincible super-spy named Avakum Zakhov, whose moral superiority over his imperialist rival is demonstrated by his preference for such wholesome proletarian fare as noodles and cabbage, instead of Bond's caviar and Dom Pérignon. Zakhov is actually pitted against 07 (a zero had to be dropped for copyright reasons) in a book selected for young readers in 1966 by the official Communist youth magazine. Spy films appear to be particularly popular in East Germany. The French weekly *L'Express* reports that when the West German authorities announced the arrest of Gunther Guillaume, the Communist spy who came in from the cold to betray the friendship of former chancellor Willy Brandt, the cultural authorities in East Berlin, presumably in homage to the captured agent, ordered a rerun of an early Communist spy thriller called *Top Secret*.

Several Western intelligence organizations appear in recent years to have been following, though more discreetly, the Communist example in acting as behind-the-scenes patrons of the arts. Both France and Britain indulge intelligence and political-police personnel who moonlight in espionage literature, and if Tad Szulc's CIA informants are to be relied upon, the agency's former head, Richard Helms, occasionally presented visitors to his office with copies of Hunt's thrillers. Even if the gesture is interpreted as an illustration of Helms's sophisticated sense of humor, it is significant that the CIA allowed Hunt to publish his tales, for they are sufficiently realistic—in spots—to give the

---

Great Gamesmen

BADEN-POWELL   WENNERSTRÖM

Some spies, perhaps the most beguiling variety of all, pursue their craft for the sheer playful derring-do of it.

Consider the case of Stig Wennerström. A World War II Swedish air force officer, the handsome, debonair Wennerström did not come into his own until the war's end. Stationed variously in Moscow, Washington, and Stockholm as a military attaché, he turned to spying and, finding it entirely to his liking, spied (1) for Sweden against Russia, (2) for Russia against Sweden, (3) for Russia against the United States, (4) for the United States against Russia, and (5) for Germany against Russia. It could hardly have been the money—some weeks he was lucky to clear $75. There was, it seems, simply something about the undercover life that appealed to him.

For the prototype of the modern gamesman-spy, however, we must look to pre-World War I England and the unlikely figure of Lord Robert Baden-Powell. Baden-Powell, who later founded the international Boy Scout movement, was a spy of such relentless zest that he once went so far as to recommend spying for its restorative powers ("For anyone who is tired of life, the thrilling life of a spy should be the very finest recuperator!"). As an international spy in the late nineteenth century, Baden-Powell learned to make a diagram of enemy fortifications look exactly like an innocent sketch of a butterfly. He also became a master of disguises, often gathering vital information by virtue of having on hand the classic butterfly net, sketchbook, and false beard. Cornered once in a railroad station, he darted into the waiting room, changed his hat, put on an overcoat, feigned a tottery invalid's shuffle, and left his baffled pursuers safely behind. "Spying," he concluded, "would be an intensely interesting sport even if no great results were obtainable from it."

---

professional reader some useful information about how its agents, and particularly their minds, operate.

Paralleling the campaign to encourage the creation of fictional spy heroes, the Kremlin has, since the early 1960's, systematically glorified the deeds of real ones. Under Stalin, and for some time after his death, the wartime services of Richard Sorge went unrecognized—no doubt because that German crypto-Communist, who became the most successful agent of the GPU (the Soviet secret military intelligence) before he died a martyr's death in a Japanese prison, had warned Stalin of Hitler's intention to attack the Soviet Union and was ignored. (Sorge's equally accurate reports that Japan would not join the Axis war against the U.S.S.R. did, however, embolden Stalin to transfer several Red Army divisions from the Soviet Far East.) But in November, 1964, shortly after Khrushchev's fall from power, Sorge was posthumously made a Hero of the Soviet Union, and an outpouring of hagiography appeared in the press, both about him and about the other previously secret combatants in the underground war against Hitler.

Less than a year later a still more remarkable revelation came to light: that Rudolf Abel, the KGB agent arrested in the United States by the FBI in 1957 (and subsequently exchanged for Francis Gary Powers, the U-2 pilot and CIA agent shot down over Soviet territory on an espionage mission), had in fact been a spy operating against American imperialism. For his good work, and particularly for his steadfast silence after his arrest, he, too, had been awarded a Soviet decoration. (Later, Powers, a good deal less deservedly, received the CIA's special medal at a formal ceremony at the agency's headquarters.) A Soviet TV feature glorified Abel's earlier services against the Nazis. In an article published by *Pravda*, the writer Vladimir Semichastny concluded: "One cannot help feeling a deep admiration and gratitude for the valiant Soviet agents, like the Hero of the Soviet Union Richard Sorge and the one known by the name of Rudolf Abel, who accomplished difficult but honorable tasks in the struggle against the enemy." Abel himself signed an article in a magazine for young Communists implicitly counseling them to think of a career in the KGB ("the best representatives of our youth are coming into the KGB") and stressing the high moral qualities needed by a Soviet agent operating in the capitalist countries: patriotic dedication, honesty, and a willingness to live in humble obscurity.

The CIA philosophy of agent recruitment, as expounded by Peter Ward— *On Hazardous Duty* again—sounds more down-to-earth. "Give me the mercenary agent over the idealist any time," he quotes one of his old instructors as saying. "The idealist is basically unreliable." Peter, it is true, is talking about recruiting *foreign* agents. It is O.K. for American agents to be a bit idealistic, as long as they have the right ideals and keep them under control. Peter himself, ever ready to risk his life for his country (or at least his country club), is dedicated enough: he can live for a day or two on C rations when he has to, but he definitely prefers lobster. His creator appears to share his taste: it will be recalled that just before the Watergate break-in attempt Hunt ordered a lobster dinner for his entire team of patriotic burglars. The check came to $236.

While the promotion of the secret agent as an official culture hero in the Warsaw Pact countries raises some troubling questions, we need not put too alarming an interpretation upon the available evidence. It may simply indicate that the KGB and the GPU are having trouble with their recruitment programs at home—an encouraging sign. Or, more speculatively, it may be that the Kremlin is preparing for increased Soviet participation in the capitalist business world, where the practice of commercial espionage and other forms of secret service skulduggery have been expanding at a spectacular rate. In the business community, too, the secret agent seems to be turning into a culture hero.

Deeds of Derring-Don't

HAYHANEN

The hero of spy fiction is fearless, obedient, efficient, and clever. His real-life counterparts may enjoy some of these James Bondian virtues, but consider the careers of Heinrich Albert, George Davis, Richard Bissell, and Reino Hayhanen—bumblers all.

Albert, a German spy in New York prior to World War I, was expert at budgeting covert operations but innocent of Manhattan. It was on an elevated train that he met his Waterloo. He neglected his briefcase full of sabotage plans only for a moment, but as every New Yorker knows, a moment is enough: a U.S. agent snatched it and just disappeared.

Davis, né Dasch, left America for his native Germany in 1941 and returned the next year on a U-boat that deposited him and three other agents on a Long Island beach. Six days later he got cold feet and turned himself and his companions in to the FBI. Davis and one of his comrades went to prison; the rest were executed.

Bissell, an economist turned CIA man, seems to have been pursued by bad luck. Involved in the information-gathering programs that launched the inglorious U-2 incident, he went on to administer the most embarrassing fizzle of all: the Bay of Pigs invasion. Dedicated service did not stand him in good stead, and he was fired.

But for sheer ineptitude, few spies can match Reino Hayhanen, a Soviet agent in the U.S. in the 1950's. His superior, the redoubtable Colonel Rudolf Abel, was a topnotch professional, but Hayhanen knew nothing about spying—and next to nothing about photography, even though his cover was a Newark, New Jersey, photo shop. Hayhanen was finally recalled to Moscow, but Abel's relief was short-lived: en route, Hayhanen defected to U.S. authorities and served as the main witness against his former boss.

What historic forces underlie this sinister trend? How and where did it start?

Historically, the mystique of the secret agent has grown out of two centuries of revolutionary turmoil and national (or imperial) power struggles. Culturally, it reflects the mental pollutants spewed by an increasingly disordered industrial civilization, pollutants that we unwittingly absorb along with our daily rations of DDT, radioactive fallout, and atmospheric lead.

The second question—how and where did it start—is less complicated, but the answer is ironic. The century that gave birth to the modern dream of the open society—the eighteenth—and the land where it first took practical shape—America—also witnessed the beginnings of the secret agent cult, glorifying an activity that today constitutes a deadly threat to the open society. The person who launched the cult was our first woman professional writer and historian, Hannah Adams (1755-1831). In her *Summary History of New England* she related a half-forgotten incident of the Revolutionary War that, thanks to her, has been an American schoolbook anthology piece ever since: the intelligence mission behind the British lines undertaken by a patriotic young Yale graduate named Nathan Hale; his arrest and hanging; and his immortal, defiant statement to his executioners: "I only regret that I have but one life to lose for my country."

It was, of course, as a patriot rather than a spy that Hannah Adams mythologized Hale; she displays virtually no interest in the craft of spying. Nevertheless, the elevation of a spy to the role of national hero marks a milestone in the evolution of Western attitudes toward secret service activity (and suggests that nationalism is the enemy behind the enemy of the open society). Spies and secret agents have, of course, been used throughout history, and individual spies have sometimes been ennobled or otherwise honored for their work. But the spy's profession has almost always and everywhere been regarded with contempt. "Espionage is never tolerable," wrote Montesquieu. "The necessary infamy of the practitioner establishes the infamous nature of the practice." The one example of a society in which spies seem to have enjoyed social esteem is hardly encouraging. According to the French anthropologist Jacques Soustelle, the incorrigibly expansionist rulers of the ancient Aztec empire habitually used merchant travelers to spy on neighboring states—much as the CIA is said to use American firms operating abroad today and the KGB to use Soviet trade delegations. In recognition of their services, members of the Aztec merchants' corporation were honored as "uncles" of the emperor.

The French Revolution and the Napoleonic Wars gave the secret agent a role of unprecedented importance and produced a number of figures, more or less closely connected with the espionage world, whose lives may strike us today as romantic. (With the possible exception of Wellington's secret intelligence officer Lieutenant Colonel Colquhoun Grant, however, they seldom *looked* particularly romantic.) And it was—once again—an American writer, James Fenimore Cooper, who first endowed the spy figure with an intriguing aura of romance.

Cooper's novel *The Spy*, published in 1821 and said to have been based on a Revolutionary War anecdote related to him by John Jay, follows the example of Hannah Adams in stressing the patriotic—that is, nationalist—motif, but he draws no veil over the sordid aspects of espionage work. His hero, Harvey Birch, is in fact very close to the double agents that haunt the pages of such modern masters of ambiguity as John le Carré. He deliberately encourages the suspicion that he is spying for the British, the better to conceal his activities as an American spy. All true patriots despise him. Only Washington knows that Harvey Birch is the truest patriot of them all.

The atmosphere of ambiguity, the attention given to disguise and other details of the craft, and the startling appearance of Washington himself in the role of spy-master (the archetype of Ashenden's chief, "R," Bond's "M," A. L. Dominique's *le vieux,* and similar figures in countless other spy stories) make *The Spy* an authentic ancestor of the modern espionage novel. But it is much more than that. It is the first appearance of the mythical theme that underlies not only the espionage novel but the whole modern cult of the secret agent: the theme of the covert hero and his arcane apotheosis.

It is because Harvey Birch's heroism has to be concealed that he is so heroic. Like every other secret agent (at least in literature), he has to forgo the hero's normal reward of having his prowess recognized. Indeed, he stoically accepts the shame of being viewed as a traitor. For Harvey, even the hope of posthumous rehabilitation is uncertain. "Remember that the veil which conceals your true character cannot be raised in years—perhaps ever," Washington warns him. The spy's only reward comes in this last interview with his chief, in the hand that the Virginia aristocrat holds out to the humble peddler, in the look of respect he has earned from the one man on earth who knows his secret.

A century and a quarter following the publication of Cooper's novel, we find the same theme set forth in the public tribute paid by General Donovan to his wartime subordinates in the OSS: "The performance of these individuals . . . is the more worthy of commendation because it was undertaken with the express understanding that their heroism might have to remain unsung. They accepted their dangerous missions, knowing that if they were killed in the line of duty their widows or children perhaps would never learn the nature of the missions for which they volunteered."

There is unquestionably a moral element, a kind of stoic idealism, in the myth of the covert hero that is imbedded in the modern image of the secret agent, but it has been increasingly adulterated by other elements since Cooper's day—and even since Donovan's.

Some of the adulterating influences were already apparent in early nineteenth-century society and were noted by Cooper's great French contemporary Balzac. Though Balzac's novels are thought of as precursors of the modern crime story rather than of the espionage novel, his enigmatic police-chief criminal, Vautrin (based on the still more enigmatic real-life Vidocq), typifies the *déclassé* adventurer destined to become before long a key figure in the secret service landscape. Vautrin-Vidocq, master of disguise and supreme exemplar of what the French literary sociologist Roger Caillois calls "that diabolical invention, the invisible police," incarnates, moreover, several of the chthonic traits subsequently found in the mythic personality of the secret agent: his ambiguous role as lawless servant of the lawful sovereign state, his Robin Hood charm, his subtle incantation of black magic and primitive tribal rites that lurk in our collective unconscious.

It was Balzac, finally, who put his unerring finger on one of the basic motivations of the secret agent in every age, one of the essential sources of his imaginative appeal: "The trade of a spy is a very fine one . . . is it not enjoying the excitements of a thief, while retaining the character of an honest citizen?"

All the forces of change left their mark on the emergent secret service mythology: the transformation of eighteenth-century patriotism into the more delusive nationalism of the nineteenth and twentieth centuries; changes in the structure of Western capitalism (particularly the decay of its traditions and ethical codes); the rise of colonial imperialism and the increase of international and social tensions in the last decades of the nineteenth century. Of even more direct importance was the professionalization of secret service activity in the leading European powers, initiated by Bismarck's great spy-master Wilhelm Stieber and culminating early in the twentieth century with the establishment of the two British secret services—

the Secret Intelligence Service, MI6, and the counterespionage service, MI5—as distinct government departments.

The two great wars in the second half of the nineteenth century—the American Civil War and the Franco-Prussian War—further sharpened official awareness of espionage as an essential tool of warfare and enhanced public interest in spies. Wars always do. The American conflict produced two particularly colorful figures: Allan Pinkerton, the paleo-private eye who became Lincoln's secret service chief, and Rose Greenhow, a popular Washington hostess who managed to collect a good deal of useful information for the Confederates before Pinkerton's sleuths caught up with her. Though Mrs. Greenhow was one of the early Delilahs of modern espionage, her success appears to have been the result of her social graces and sharp mind rather than her beauty. In the Franco-Prussian War Stieber sent a whole army of spies ahead of the Prussian uniformed forces. It was the first example in the history of espionage of the mass saturation technique later employed by Hitler, and it seemed to the French a fiendish innovation. (The recognition of the fiend in the enemy spy has loomed large in popular attitudes toward espionage: by a kind of magical transference, the fiendish traits of the enemy almost invariably come to be incorporated in the idealized image of the secret agent—one's own, that is; being a bit of a fiend becomes part of his charm.)

It was in the Afro-Asian colonies of the leading European powers, however, that the secret service tradition and myth grew most rapidly. The British metropolitan secret services—MI6 and MI5—were largely staffed at the beginning by old professionals from India, the only part of the Empire where such professionals existed in any number, and both were lastingly stamped by this colonialist influence. The secret agent is even more an imperialist than a nationalist culture hero. It was in India, specifically, that espionage first became the Great Game, as Kipling called it in *Kim*, an early and typical spy story,

Two for the Money

"Cicero"   Mata Hari

For some spies, the only thing that really counts is payday.

Take the legendary Mata Hari, a seductive exotic dancer who was responsible for perhaps fifty thousand Allied deaths in World War I. Trained at a German espionage school, the Dutch-born enchantress was sent to Paris at the outbreak of the war. There, as her willowy charms ingratiated her in diplomatic and military circles, some people began to notice a curiously persistent connection between what her new friends told her and the military mishaps that thereafter befell the Allies. In time, hoping to make the best of a bad thing, France offered her a job as a double agent. Handing her a list of spies in Belgium, they asked her to fetch their intelligence reports. Replied Mata Hari ingratiatingly: "I am proud to do this for the France that I love." Ever the opportunist, she promptly sold the list to the Germans, who methodically began to eliminate the Belgian agents. Even for the tolerant French, that was a bit much: they executed Mata Hari by firing squad.

A World War II spy, Elyesa Bazna—better known by his code name "Cicero"—was the victim of a similar acquisitiveness but a different misfortune. A brooding, mistrustful Yugoslav ("There is no such thing as loyalty and trust in this game"), Cicero drifted from one job to another before finding fulfillment as a German spy in the British embassy in Ankara. Beginning in 1943, he photographed countless valuable documents—among them Normandy invasion plans, which his suspicious employers chose, to their later regret, to ignore—always receiving top dollar for his pains. "Whenever I felt misgivings," he wrote, "I laid my hands on the money. . . . I was a wealthy man." But the Germans had the last laugh. All along, they had been paying him in counterfeit money.

though it seems strange to think of such a magical literary creation in those terms. As Hannah Arendt observes in *The Origins of Totalitarianism*, the amoral concept of spying as a game played for its own sake reflects a typical attitude of the *déclassé* or socially marginal adventurer who is one of its most commonly encountered players. I think, however, that she underestimates the element of sheer professionalism behind it. To the secret service professional—the respectable sedentary bureaucrat no less than the agent in the field—espionage (or counterespionage) is a fascinating game of wits. The ludic element is particularly likely to be uppermost—or very close behind the imperatives of duty and country—when the game involves foreign rivals and indigenous subversion on the colonial field. The stakes, though high, do not necessarily involve the nation's very existence, and the pawns—the operating agents—since they are usually "natives," are by definition expendable.

Whether the Great Game spirit filtered from the colonies into the metropolitan headquarters of the major European spy services, or whether it had roots at home as well, it became a dominant trait of the secret service mind in the half-century before World War I. Naturally, it was most pronounced in the English—the sporting, as well as the imperial, race par excellence.

One of the most enthusiastic eulogizers of the Great Game as a fascinating and character-building sport was Kipling's friend Lord Robert Baden-Powell, the founder (in 1908) of the international Boy Scout movement. Though most of his military career was spent as a fighting colonial soldier, he took time off for the odd intelligence mission, in Africa, Turkey, and elsewhere. He sometimes adopted the cover of an amateur entomologist, complete with butterfly net, as an excuse for loitering near enemy military objectives he wished to sketch, thus launching the silly-ass tradition that was long cultivated in the British SIS. "Spying," Baden-Powell wrote in his memoirs, *My*

Adventures as a Spy, "would be an intensely interesting sport even if no great results were obtainable from it. There is a fascination which gets hold of anyone who has tried the art." Except when they are traitors to their country, Baden-Powell declared, spies are honorable, brave, and generally admirable fellows. He even voiced admiration for German spies, at least the better class of German spy, though his book was published in 1915.

The Great Game ethos of the professionals was reflected in the spy novels (and a little later in the films) whose true vogue, despite the success of Cooper's pioneer work, dates only from the 1890's. (*Kim* appeared in 1901.) The man generally credited with having launched the vogue was William Le Queux (true name: Tufnell), 1864–1927, a British journalist who is said, on somewhat uncertain authority, to have been a secret agent himself and to have turned out popular fiction to eke out the meager operational budget allowed him by his chiefs in the nascent British intelligence service. Le Queux, soon followed by such once-famous clubland and circulating-library stars as Erskine Childers, E. Phillips Oppenheim, and John Buchan, contributed another essential touch of romance to the modern image of the secret agent. Unlike the raffish barracks-waif Kim and his associates in the Great Game—the Afghan horse dealer Mahbub Ali, the caricatural Bengali Hurree Babu, the not-quite-*pukka* Lurgan Sahib—their heroes are generally well-born and often wealthy young English amateurs, while their villains—diplomats, decadent Continental aristocrats—are surrounded with the glamour of high-level iniquity. (The Dreyfus Affair in France —which inspired two early films—and the exposure of Colonel Alfred Redl, the Austrian secret service chief, as a traitor working for the Russians were both potent stimulants to the romantic imagination.) From the readers' point of view, the moral of the spy novels was that a career in the secret service offered at once an opportunity to serve one's country

gloriously, to have thrilling adventures, and to mingle with the very best—or most fascinatingly wicked—people.

The myth of espionage as an essentially patrician sport, like polo, had some slight foundation. In the early twentieth century secret service budgets (except possibly in Russia) were still modest, and to stretch them as far as possible the professionals often had to rely on unpaid, part-time helpers, motivated by patriotism or the love of adventure and recruited in the higher levels of society. The French, especially in colonial areas, made extensive use of such volunteer informants among certain of the missionary orders. The British SIS early began recruiting promising Oxford and Cambridge undergraduates, sometimes merely for vacation espionage jaunts of the butterfly-catching type, sometimes as full-time professionals. T. E. Lawrence, according to Philip Knightley and Colin Simpson in *The Secret Lives of Lawrence of Arabia,* was introduced to the Great Game by his Oxford patron, the well-known scholar D. G. Hogarth, during summer archaeological outings in Turkey.

As the secret services of the great powers acquired ever increasing importance in our century of technological and political revolution, the bureaucrats who ran them became more respectable in the eyes of their colleagues, and the espionage establishment tended to merge with the Establishment. The trend, as usual, was most marked in England. The World War II head of MI6, its legendary "C," Major General Sir Stewart Graham Menzies, was a member of White's, one of the two most prestigious clubs in the kingdom; as the authors of *The Philby Conspiracy* remark, his fellow members saw nothing odd in his conducting a significant part of his department's business from White's bar and dining room. And as Le Carré writes in his brilliant introduction to the book, that clubby British attitude was one of the key reasons why Philby's treason was not uncovered much sooner.

The OSS and the early CIA inherited

some of MI6's snob appeal. Though tarnished by various scandals—in England above all by the Philby case—the secret service hero still keeps a stiff upper lip socially. James Bond is no longer received in Society as Buchan's or Childers's heroes were—where is there a Society to be received into?—but he is thoroughly at home in café society, and even though what Peter Ward calls his "Cape Codding" sounds a trifle unconvincing, preliminary research indicates that he does order his riding boots from the right suburb of Buenos Aires. His plumbing tools come from a first-class supplier, too.

The First World War vastly enhanced the secret agent's heroic stature and romantic prestige, but nowhere, except on the revolutionary front in Russia, did it add much of anything to the already well-established image of the patriot-ready-to-die-as-an-unsung-hero, the master of ruse and disguise, the Great Gamesman, and the aristocrat-by-association. Lawrence was easily the most romantic incarnation of the ideal, but if Lawrence's guerrilla campaign in the desert was an epic, it was more of a military than a secret service epic; and though the brooding sense of betrayal and self-betrayal that hangs over his *Seven Pillars of Wisdom* reflects a typical secret agent's *Weltschmerz*, it is likewise that of every adventurous dreamer who sees his dream come halfway true.

It was the Second World War that gave the secret agent one of his most significant new traits since Cooper's day: the James Bond look, the look of violence. He became not merely a spy but a saboteur, a killer, an organizer of resistance networks, a ruthless guerrilla chief. The savage colonial or semi-colonial wars, declared and undeclared, that have marked the history of the last thirty years—Indochina, Korea, Algeria, the Near East, and Indochina again—have further accentuated the element of violence, both in the secret agent's real professional activity and in his public image. All these conflicts have been more or less closely linked with the global power struggle between the United States and the Soviet Union (though most of them had autogenous roots), and the direct confrontations between their rival secret services have sometimes been equally savage—especially in the vital Central European sector. Before World War II the professionals occasionally assassinated one another's human pawns in the Great Game—"natives," foreign agents, low-level subagents—but almost never their own opposite numbers. At the height of the Cold War, however, such fratricidal attacks became one of the secret service officer's recognized—if still relatively minor—occupational hazards, something akin to a secret service vendetta developed at times, and casualties among the pawns attained unprecedented levels all over the world.

Vietnam was an example. There the pawns included not merely secret service, police, and paramilitary personnel on both sides, but the enemy's political infrastructure, from the hamlet level to as high as the assassin's arm could reach. Terrorist attacks on "collaborationist" officials in enemy-occupied territory, carried out by the resistance underground with the help of Allied secret services, had been common enough in World War II—and had been enthusiastically applauded by public opinion in the democracies when they became known; but what went on in Vietnam was worse than mass terrorism: it was a kind of systematic political genocide. On what most Americans thought of as "our" side, it was conducted by Saigon assassination squads, and in part organized by the CIA.

Until American opponents of the Vietnam War began lifting corners of the veil, the public was poorly informed, to say the least, about the savageries perpetrated by our side. (Communist atrocities were, of course, well publicized.) Even if it had been known from the start how our secret agents were defending the rule of law and of Christian civilization, it probably would not have tarnished their image in the American public mind. It might even have added romantic luster. James Bond and his fictional colleagues of the Cold War period did not acquire their popularity by preaching nonviolence, though of course when they kill or torture it is always in reprisal for some fiendishness committed by the enemy. (In war, hot or cold, it always is.) Moreover, the revolutionary terrorists, one of the secret agent's most serious rivals as a modern culture hero, especially among the young, seems to become more romantic with each massacre of innocent people.

So we come to a moral feature of the contemporary secret agent that is no less essential than his look of violence: his personification, in his role as a political conspirator, of the ideological crusader. This aspect of his character, which, like his violence, attained its full development during the Cold War, also dates from World War II.

The ideological conspirator role was not, of course, strictly new. A striking example from World War I was Sidney Reilly, the Russian-born SIS agent who after the Bolshevik Revolution organized a series of insurrectionary plots against the new regime and nearly succeeded in having Lenin assassinated before mysteriously disappearing himself in the course of a last, patently doomed underground mission. He was a full staff member of the SIS, but he was rarely content to carry out his British chief's instructions; consumed by an almost demented hatred of Communism, he often exceeded, and sometimes totally ignored, them.

Reilly, however, was an extreme case. In the 1930's the ideological conspirator—fascist or antifascist, Communist or anti-Communist—became a standard feature of the European political landscape, sometimes co-operating with the police or intelligence services of his own country against those he considered its enemies, sometimes working against them because he considered them in league with the enemy, sometimes merely keeping distrustfully aloof from them. There are reflections of this attitude in the new kind of espionage novel that writers like Eric Ambler and Graham Greene turned out during the period. Their heroes sometimes found themselves caught up in the Great Game, but they rarely thought of themselves as playing it—or, rather, it had ceased to be a game.

It was Munich that told all Western democrats that espionage was no longer a game. They had previously viewed Hitler's new Germany as representing a conventional but not-to-be-exaggerated military threat to democracy; Munich declared it a monstrous, worldwide enterprise of subversion. What it sought to subvert was as much a set of moral values as a political ideology or a national loyalty, and many of those susceptible to its propaganda seemed to become its accomplices without quite realizing what they were doing. The fall of France, which to those who witnessed it (as I did) seemed no less a political and psychological collapse than a military one, naturally confirmed this almost demonological view of the Nazi menace. No doubt the interpretation was excessive and a bit irrational, but it helps explain why a certain number of Americans at the time began to think of confronting what they regarded as the Nazi conspiracy in the United States with counterconspiracy.

In an effort to change what was still the United States policy of neutrality, some of my friends with too little faith in their fellow citizens and in the normal processes of American democracy began working with organizations that they knew to be financed and controlled by the British. A few, convinced that they were acting in the interests of the nation itself, even became actual British agents, conspiring against the laws of their country. I might have ended by doing the same if, in the desperate summer of 1941, the creation of General Donovan's embryonic intelligence service, soon to become the OSS, had not offered me the chance to conspire legally against the foreign enemy. Or at least to conspire officially, if not always legally.

Looking-glass Warriors

PHILBY

In the nether world of espionage, a particular odium—and with it a particular fascination—attaches to that distorted mirror image of the patriotic spy known as the double agent. One notorious exemplar of the breed was Colonel Alfred Redl, who, in the opening years of this century, directed intelligence-gathering operations for the Austro-Hungarian Empire. Redl, a brilliant innovator, pioneered such techniques as photographing visitors with concealed cameras, obtaining their fingerprints without their knowledge, and recording their words on hidden wax cylinders. In May, 1913, however, he was finally revealed to be a Russian agent and shot himself: the Russians, it turned out, had discovered ten years before that Redl was a homosexual and had blackmailed him into co-operating with them. A year later, when Austria-Hungary attacked Russia's ally, Serbia, the Russians' knowledge of the plan of attack may have been responsible for the deaths of as many as a quarter of a million invaders.

The most celebrated double agent of all time is alive to this very day. He is, of course, Harold ("Kim") Philby, the suave, worldly, upper-middle-class graduate of Westminster and Cambridge who joined the British Secret Intelligence Service in 1940 and in 1963 defected to the Soviet Union, for which he had, in fact, been working all those years. Like his fellow double agents, Guy Burgess and Donald Maclean, Philby had embraced Communism in his youth and remained ever after an enemy of the British Establishment in which he had been raised and which he ostensibly served. Even in the cozier political climate of Moscow, however, Philby showed little inclination to mend his duplicitous ways: he made off with his friend Maclean's wife.

Like Peter Ward (and his inventor) thirty years later, my OSS comrades and I had few scruples about becoming lawless in the struggle to uphold the law.

One likes to think that the antifascist fanaticism that helped tempt some of us into secret service work in 1940 and 1941 was less ugly than the atmosphere of moral nihilism that overhangs the—in some ways—analogous activities of the Nixon plumbers. A similar plea could no doubt be made for the equally fanatical—and equally sincere—anti-Stalinism that lured a certain number of liberals into the CIA during the agency's early years, before the American secret service ethos had degenerated into the cryptoimperialist dream of world policemanship and economic hegemony, and, if recent revelations can be trusted, into the obsessive dread not merely of revolution but of any social change anywhere. But fanatics, no matter how high-minded, are generally blind to the contradictions between the ends they pursue and the means they employ, and I fear that many of the conspiratorial squalors of the present were implicit in the conspiratorial idealisms of the past.

Two things in particular—both essential elements of the secret agent mystique in its democratic version—misled a number of us during the struggle, first against the Nazi, then against Stalinist, totalitarianism. One was the heady feeling of belonging to an elite of secret guardians of the republic. We failed to reflect that republics so guarded in the past have generally turned into empires. The other error was the belief that because the republic appeared to be—and probably was—threatened by subversion, it could only be saved by conspiracy.

For conspiracy, whether practiced at home or abroad, for private advantage or for what is conceived to be the public welfare, becomes a habit that grows on those who practice it. As we have seen.

Historian Edmond Taylor has contributed articles to HORIZON *on Trotsky, Camoëns, and Dreyfus; on May Day and terrorism; and on international freedom movements.*

How Republics Die

What kills representative governments? It is not always the mob

It is one of the revealing curiosities of history that the founders of the American Republic were none too sanguine about the viability of republican government. Some of them feared that the new republic might fall under the sway of a despot raised to power by the ignorant masses; others, that it might be subverted by an oligarchy of the privileged. These were, and still are, deeply considered and honorable, though contradictory, views. The citizens who hold one or the other might, in fact, be thought of as constituting the two real and enduring parties in any republic, whatever the official views of the official political parties might be.

In the unending debate between these groups, those who fear mob-inspired despotism have always enjoyed one powerful intellectual advantage, for the history of classical antiquity bears out—indeed, has done much to inspire—their fear. In ancient Greece and republican Rome it was emphatically and repeatedly the patrician class that defended republican institutions and the mob, through its chosen tyrant, that subverted them. Republican Cato and imperious Caesar define the classic confrontation, but dozens of lesser Catos and lesser Caesars had played similar roles before them in the Greek city-states.

Yet there is another notable chapter in the annals of republics that tells a different tale, a tale in which the destroyers are not the mob but the privileged. That chapter narrates the complex and tragic history of the vanished city-states of medieval Italy.

They began to emerge, these tiny mu-

nicipal upstarts, in northern and central Italy—Lombardy and Tuscany—during the eleventh century, when scarcely a trace of ancient republicanism was left in Western Christendom. Pisa was the first to establish a formal government, an executive commission of "consuls," appropriating the title of ancient Rome's most exalted officials. This usage, soon adopted by neighboring towns, represented a deliberate attempt to bestow authority on their precarious governments, for in theory feudal order

A flawed republic dies: in this detail from a fresco, Archbishop Ottone Visconti enters Milan in 1277 after routing the Della Torre clan, despots who had seized power in the name of the people.

ruled over all, and the towns, or "communes" as contemporary Italians called them, had no authority whatever.

Thus the communes were not only upstarts but also political usurpers. To the extent that a new commune won jurisdiction over the people of a diocese, it usurped the power of the local bishop; insofar as it pushed its rule into the countryside, it usurped the authority of some feudal magnate; when it engaged

in war or diplomacy with its neighbors, it defied the Holy Roman Emperor—the supreme ruler, in theory, of every member of every commune. Like woodsmen felling trees, the men of the commune were clearing a space for municipal liberty in the vast forest of feudalism. By the middle of the twelfth century there were some three hundred such communes, energetically enlarging their jurisdictions, pinching the power of bishops, dukes, and marquises, and ignoring the Holy Roman Emperor the moment his armies left Italy. Their victory over the feudality astonished all who knew of it. A Jewish traveler reported in the twelfth century: "They possess neither king nor prince to govern them, but only the judges appointed by themselves."

Outwardly at least, communes were utterly new organisms and their inhabitants utterly new men. Between the surrounding feudal order and the civil society of a city-state there is scarcely a point of resemblance. In the former, all ties among people are personal; in the latter, men find their primary bond through living together in a common territory under a common law. Under feudalism, a crime is a personal affront to be avenged by the victim's family; in a city-state, it is an offense against the community, punishable only by its magistrates. In the feudal order people rule because rule is their birthright; in communes, they rule by consent of their fellow inhabitants.

In establishing republican communities the men of the communes had to do more than merely triumph over the surrounding feudality: they also had to extirpate the feudal ethos itself. They

By WALTER KARP

never quite succeeded in doing this. If, as Aristotle said, a free city is one whose members are "able to rule and to obey in turn," then the fatal flaw in the Italian city-states was the refusal of those who ruled to take their turn at obeying.

Although from the earliest days the communes had popular institutions of government—usually large, elective councils—power rested for a long time with men of noble birth and knightly titles, the *maiores,* in the parlance of the commune, as distinct from the *populares,* the people. The knights of the communes were by no means great lords, and most of them were happy to make money in trade; they had, as a rule, joined their destinies to that of the new communes to escape from vassalage to the dukes and counts of the surrounding countryside.

Within the towns, however, knights expected—like any feudal lord—to rule by right of birth: escaping vassalage themselves, they did not scruple to re-establish vassalage in the towns and to walk the streets of their cities with armed retinues in their train. While the plain people strove to strengthen the city courts, the *maiores* held to the family law of revenge, as if the city's civil jurisdiction were fit only for the rabble. Civic patriotism and public spirit left them unmoved: they were as likely to betray as to further their own commune's ambitions vis-à-vis its rivals. Ensconced in fortified town houses, waging civil war in the streets among themselves like the gangs of Prohibition Era Chicago, the nobles of the communes looked upon the communal government either as an instrument for family advancement (when their own family controlled it) or as a sword to be blunted should a rival family hold it in its grasp.

The true "new men" of the communes were not its rulers but the people themselves. It was they who defended the common law and stood by the government, shedding their blood in its cause, when the feuding nobles were tearing it apart. As P. J. Jones, a leading modern authority on the Italian city-states, has noted, "it was the populares, despised

and misruled by their betters, who understood the meaning of civic virtue and the true requirements of republican government and did so long before the humanists of Florence began studying republicanism in the texts of classical antiquity."

Though they were far from meek and hapless, there is genuine pathos in the *populares'* fidelity to law and in their faith in legalistic contrivances. When the internecine warfare among the nobles had all but destroyed the consulate, the people created a new municipal officer, the *podestà*—a sort of city manager chosen from another city for a fixed term of office in the hope that a paid official from a neutral quarter would administer municipal affairs in a professional manner and thereby overawe the nobility. But the ruling families were too strong and too contemptuous of law for such a feeble constitutional makeshift to have much of an effect.

The *populares,* however, were undaunted. If the civil government was too weak to curb the insolence of the "magnates," as they were now called, there was nothing to do, popular leaders decided, but organize the people themselves as the active arm of the government. In almost all the Italian city-states the *populares* formed groups known as *popolos,* each headed by an elected captain and council. Backed by its own militia drawn from all the wards of the city, the *popolo* of every commune dedicated itself to upholding the communal government—by arms if necessary—and to curbing the insolence of the magnates.

With that, the fates began to close in on the free city-states of Italy. In Lombardy, the resurgence of the people was more than the nobility could stomach, even though it was their own profound contempt for republican institutions that had brought that resurgence about. A choice was now put before them: to share power with the despised *populares* or to surrender their power to some feudal magnate who would rule the city as a despot but at least protect their privi-

leges. The magnates chose the privileges—and political impotence. With that choice, municipal liberty in northern Italy was virtually snuffed out by the end of the thirteenth century. The powerful Visconti family became the despots of Milan. The counts of Montefeltro made Urbino their fiefdom. The D'Estes took over Ferrara and Mantua, the Scaliger family came to dominate Verona. Soon the forest of feudalism had grown back over a good half of the little world of the Italian city-states.

Even where the *popolos* proved stronger than the nobility—in Pisa, Siena, and Florence, for example—the refusal of the mighty to "obey in turn" eventually did its work of ruination. Though technically members of the *popolo,* the great Tuscan merchants and bankers—"the fat people," their fellow citizens called them—proved as determined to rule as the older nobility had been, and as loath to share power. By subverting the constitution, rigging elections, and suppressing dissent, the new magnates turned the republican institutions of their cities into hollow and meaningless forms.

In the fifteenth century the city-states of Tuscany, like those of Lombardy before them, succumbed one by one to a tyranny scarcely distinguishable from the oligarchy it replaced. Finally, when Florence became the proprietary domain of a Medici "duke of Florence" in 1531, the Italian experiment in republican self-government came to its definitive end. It had hung on bravely for five centuries.

Is there a lesson in the story? One political observer thought so. The lesson for him was that it is the men of privilege and influence who are likely to harm, and the people who are surest to defend, republican institutions. "The demands of a free people," he noted, "are rarely pernicious to liberty." That is not the maxim of a sentimental American Jeffersonian. It is the somber conclusion of Niccolò Machiavelli as he looked back, in the bitterness of blighted republican hopes, on the "wasted world," as he called it, of vanquished republican Italy.

The Pleasures of Tapestry

Once only decorative insulation,
tapestry came to embody the visions of great
masters. Here, a poet reports on this
historic — and still flourishing — art form

The weaver in the fifteenth-century miniature above works brightly colored wool to make a delicate leaf-and-flower design. Woven in similar fashion a full five centuries later, the tapestry at left was commissioned in 1970 for a reception hall in 'sHertogenbosch, Holland. Its creator, the Polish artist Magdalena Abakanowicz, stands dwarfed by her enormous work, measuring some 65 by 26 feet.

I t is nearly twenty years since I first went up to Oxford, but even then the city produced annually more bicycles and pots of marmalade than scholars. Since I was young and snobbish, I deeply mourned the fact that this was not the Oxford of which my father had told me. Nevertheless, the colleges, the gray stone fortresses where ancient bells sang through the rain-washed air on the stroke of the hours, were changeless, and within the colleges lived certain people who still preserved a formal, rather beautiful style of life forgotten elsewhere. Nevill Coghill, a senior English professor, was one of them.

He lived in Merton, the oldest Oxford college, in a large set of very elegant, very comfortable rooms. Here, on a fixed day every week, his undergraduate friends would come to sip sherry

By DOM MORAES

Fragment, fifth or sixth century

Heroes, Unicorns, and a Sugared Almond

Tapestry weaving probably came to medieval Europe by way of the eastern Mediterranean region. There, in the fifth or sixth century, the tapestry piece at left was made. Why the gentleman is drawing back the curtain we do not know, but the figure's stylized pose turns up again centuries later in the work of European weavers. By the end of the fourteenth century, princes were commissioning vast sets of tapestries that dealt with themes from history and mythology. In a detail from one such series, The Heroes, *at right, a frowning King Arthur sits majestically on his throne. In a panel from another famous set, illustrating the five senses, opposite left, a demure lady surrounded by fanciful creatures accepts a sugared almond from her servant. Filled with equally exquisite but more realistic detail is the tapestry, opposite right, of peasants hunting in a woodland setting.*

From The Heroes, *c. 1375*

and discuss literature. Nevill was kind and witty and civilized, and his rooms were a restful place to be. Hanging on the walls between deep ogival windows were sixteenth-century Flemish tapestries. Their backgrounds had turned to a delicate pastel over the years, and gowned and veiled ladies moved across them midst flowers, fountains, and heraldic beasts. They held my eye always.

The flowered lawns on which the ladies walked seemed to extend beyond the tapestry, so that each tapestry took on the dimensions of a dream. The texture of the fabric itself, of warp and woof, seemed warmer than the texture of paint. Until then, I had seen tapestries only in museums and thought of them as being enlarged versions of the woolen samplers old English ladies put up on their parlor walls. But tapestries seen in an inhabited room, tapestries used as a part of daily life, had a quite different quality. Nevill, his finger tips moving slowly across their fabric, told me that tapestries had been hung as wall ornaments for thousands of years and now I could see why. I felt I could step into one and disappear.

*I*t is precisely because tapestry is a decorative form of art—beautiful to look at, easy to live with, removed from reality—that it was so popular for so many centuries in so many parts of the world. Because many famous tapestries were produced after the thirteenth century in Flanders and France, people often assume the craft started there. But that isn't true. Tapestries were made long before the thirteenth century, and they were made in places far removed from western Europe by craftsmen who spoke no French.

Caves and primitive huts must have been exceptionally drafty places to live in. Presumably, at some remote time, our ancestors discovered that to hang an animal hide over the entrance made pneumonia in the family less likely. If drafts still

came in through the patchwork walls of your hut, you hung hides over those as well and insulated yourself from the elements. Fabrics eventually replaced hides, and an aesthetic element entered the business of keeping yourself warm: made from colored threads and woven into patterns, the fabrics became a decoration as much as a necessity.

Egyptian friezes dating back to 3000 B.C. show horizontal looms on which tapestry was woven, and during the period of the New Kingdom vertical looms came into use. It is on these two types of loom that tapestry is still made, and, though each has its advantages and drawbacks, the end product is the same. Penelope, faithfully weaving her endless tapestry through the pages of the *Odyssey* while her husband cavorted with Circe, worked, a recent French translator of Homer says, at a vertical loom. The material she used was probably wool; the Egyptians, from the corroded scraps of tapestry found in the tombs of Amenhotep II and Tutankhamon, seem to have worked linen or the ubiquitous cotton of the delta.

In time, fabrics became more sophisticated, like the world, but the technique of tapestry weaving has always stayed much the same. On a vertical, or high-warp loom, the threads of the warp are drawn taut between the loom's top and bottom rollers, forming the background on which the whole tapestry is woven. The craftsman has a cartoon of the required design, and he places himself before the warp like a painter before a canvas, except that the wrong side of the tapestry faces him. Then, operating shuttles, he makes his design upon the warp with the cross threads, the woof, sometimes but not always using a different kind of fiber. In the finished product, the colored cobweb of the woof completely covers the warp, both front and back.

Ancient accounts speak of massive tapestries on palace walls in Babylon and Nineveh, and the Romans, too, used tapestry for decorative purposes. But the craft was by no means confined to Europe and the Middle East. Bright scraps of material

"Taste," from The Lady with the Unicorn, *15th century*

Rabbit-Hunting with Ferrets, *c. 1460-1470*

found in coastal tombs in Peru date back to the first century A.D. These were made of cotton or of llama or vicuña wool and had geometric patterns, but in northern Peru the Indians produced tapestries that depicted the local fauna in a reasonably realistic way. They were still employed at these delicate and difficult tasks when, in the sixteenth century, the Spanish conquistadors clanked their way into the New World. The conquistadors were not especially sensitive men, but even they were awed by the Peruvian tapestries: "The cloth was finished on both sides alike," Prescott writes in *The Conquest of Peru.* "The delicacy of the texture was such as to give it the lustre of silk; and the brilliancy of the dyes excited the admiration and the envy of the European artisan. . . . The Spanish sovereigns," Prescott adds, "with all the luxuries of Europe and Asia at their command, did not disdain to use them."

By the sixteenth century tapestry was, of course, well known and widely used in the courts and castles of Europe. Some of it was Eastern tapestry that had been brought home by the crusaders, but tapestry of high quality was being made in Europe as well.

When it was first made there, and by whom, was never recorded, but the likelihood is that the first European tapestries were produced in the eleventh or twelfth centuries. It might have been known in western Europe well before that time, the Romans perhaps taking the thing itself, if not its methods of manufacture, to the countries they conquered. They may even have used it as a staple of trade. But the probability is that the crusaders brought the technique back home with them, for it was widely used in the countries through which they had passed on their way to Jerusalem.

In the Negev Desert in Israel, not far from the roads down which the crusaders came, I once visited a Bedouin encampment. The chief of the tribe was called Sheik Suleiman, and hanging on the walls of his tent were assorted photographs of him taken with various notables, including David Ben-Gurion and Eleanor Roosevelt. "My friends," the sheik said. He took us out into the scald of the sun and dust and indicated, in a paddock, some splendid Arab mares and a stallion. "My horses," he said. He pointed out an assembly of parked automobiles, smirked, and said, "My cars." He had obviously displayed his possessions in a descending scale of values, and now he pointed to a large tent and said, "My women."

Inside, there were a number of them, some working on horizontal looms and weaving rugs with geometric designs in bright colors. The crusaders must have seen hangings much like those and dragged them home across desert and sea hundreds of years ago to put on their castle walls.

*T*he Coptic Christians of Egypt and Syria helped spread tapestry weaving in the Middle East. They modernized the ancient tradition of the pharaohs, and from the third century on wove tapestries, often with a linen warp and a woolen woof. The little of it that has survived shows that they were able to achieve a relief effect in much of their work through a fastidious use of shading and hatching. These were techniques that were later employed by European weavers, but one can only speculate about how they reached Europe. Nevertheless they did reach it, and around the year 1200, at some forgotten workshop in the Rhineland, the earliest tapestry known to have been made in the West, the *Cloth of Saint Gereon,* was created.

The tapestry was thought for years to be of Coptic origin, but detailed study eventually revealed its provenance as the Rhineland. It then became reasonably safe to assume that there were other workshops busy in Europe at the time and that the number increased with the demand. Tapestry was, however, not so readily available as to constitute the pride and delight of

The Miraculous Draft of Fishes, c. 1630

Angels, Harps, and a Visit from the King

Early in the sixteenth century Raphael designed a series of tapestries illustrating the lives of the Apostles for the Sistine Chapel. His designs were used many times, and in the seventeenth century the royal factory at Mortlake produced several sets. For the panel at left, based on Raphael's monumental composition of Christ and the fishermen, the Mortlake weavers made a border of mischievous angels and luscious fruits. The most famous of all royal factories was the Gobelins, organized by Louis XIV and his minister Colbert. In the tapestry designed by Charles Le Brun, opposite left, the king and Colbert arrive to inspect the products of the Gobelins, among them the tapestries that hang on the wall. The sad-eyed angels strumming harps in the tapestry opposite right were designed by the pre-Raphaelite artist Edward Burne-Jones and produced in the workshop of William Morris. The leaves and flowers in the background are a clear echo of the mille-fleurs tapestries that were woven in the fifteenth century.

every European household. A series of tapestries could take ten years to complete, and the cost could be more than an ordinary man made in a lifetime. The Church and the aristocracy were therefore almost the only customers. But in Europe during the Middle Ages there were plenty of churches and plenty of aristocrats, and the weavers didn't starve. By the middle of the thirteenth century, the art of tapestry began to flourish. In Paris, Etienne Boileau's *Livre des Métiers* (Book of Trades) recorded the existence of not just one but two guilds of tapestry weavers.

Most of the early European tapestry that has survived depicts sacred themes. Commissioned by the Church and preserved in cathedrals or convents, they remained relatively safe. The tapestries commissioned by the aristocracy were far from safe. When kings and noblemen rode to war or toured their domains, they usually carried their tapestries with them. Wherever they stopped for the night, at an inn, a friendly castle, or a tent, servants unpacked the tapestries and hung them around the walls so their masters could sleep in a womb of warm colors and familiar scenes. Pleasant as this may have been, it was hazardous: tapestries were stolen, lost, damaged, or captured by the enemy in battle.

The tapestry makers continued to thrive, particularly in Paris. In about 1375 the duke of Anjou commissioned panels of the Apocalypse from the Parisian weaver Nicolas Bataille. The completed product, designed for the chapel of the castle of Angers, was some one hundred and fifty yards long and about sixteen and a half feet high—the first really vast piece of tapestry work that we are sure was made in Europe. Others followed. The craftsmen spread out, clustering in other centers: Tournai, Brussels, and Arras, where the weavers developed a style of their own, mixing the traditional wool with silk and with threads of precious gold and silver.

After 1477, when Louis XI laid siege to Arras, Flanders became the focal point of tapestry making. New spinning and dyeing processes were developed, and the palettes of the craftsmen, once limited to a few basic colors, now became more extensive. Their reds, derived from the roots of the madder plant, and their blues, from the leaves of the woad plant, endure in the examples we have, but many of the other colors in these early tapestries have faded. This is mourned by many: I must confess that I am not one of them. The ancient Greeks and Indians were in the habit of painting their temples and statues. Now, the paint long faded from the stone, these temples and statues seem beautiful. To me, the muted colors in old tapestries are part of their beauty. They may have looked garish when new; to have appealed to the splendor-loving aristocrats of the time, they probably did.

Some very beautiful tapestries are in the Musée de Cluny in Paris, which is shady and cool even in summer. Tapestries cover its walls. When I was last there, a year ago, most of them had left for a visit to the Metropolitan Museum in New York. But there were still a lot of solemn, wimpled ladies, doubleted men, and mythological animals to stare at me. They were centuries old, and based on sources even older—the illuminated medieval manuscripts in monastery libraries. They trod the sprigged lawns of a perpetual spring. Light and color spread out over the warp and woof that had formed the figures and a landscape now lost to us all. The guards who stood about in the cool halls spoke of their charges in caressing voices. *The Lady with the Unicorn* was away, they said, in Manhattan. It seemed a curious place for her to be. But, said the guards, she would return. Indeed, when I came back to New York, she was on her way home.

This most famous tapestry of all consists of several panels and was woven in a workshop in the Loire toward the end of the fifteenth century. It is fairly typical of its period. One of the

The Visit of Louis XIV to the Gobelins in 1667

Angeli Laudantes, *1894*

panels, for example, the one illustrating the sense of taste, shows a blonde young woman in a long dress standing on a flowered oval of turf from which stiff trees sprout. A lion stands on its hind legs on one side of her, a unicorn on the other. Both carry banners. A handmaiden kneels by the lady, and a parakeet flutters on her wrist. A greyhound, an ape, and a pair of rabbits, reminiscent of Disney bunnies, play at her feet. The background of the flowered lawn on which she stands is a dull red, dappled and stippled with innumerable flowers and trees. Upon it, flattened out of perspective, are birds and, among other assorted animals, a leopard and a lioness that could only have been created by someone who had never seen a leopard or a lioness. Apart from the grave face of the lady, which, though innocent, is realistically rendered, the whole effect of the tapestry is totally unreal, and totally beautiful.

The prosperity of tapestry makers is suggested in the estimate that at the end of the fifteenth century, as the Middle Ages shambled away into history and the Renaissance made its spruce appearance, there were thousands of artisans living by the trade in and around the small town of Audenarde alone. If this was the case, the number of craftsmen in the great tapestry-making centers like Tournai, Bruges, Valenciennes, and Brussels must have been colossal. With the Renaissance, the demand for tapestries increased: now it was not only the Church and the aristocracy that wanted them, but the newly rich merchants and businessmen. Other changes took place, too, particularly in the way tapestries were designed.

In the sixteenth century painters became a real power in the world of tapestry. In 1515 Raphael was commissioned by Pope Leo X to prepare sketches for ten tapestries to illustrate the acts of the Apostles for the Sistine Chapel. Raphael completed his assignment in 1516, the cartoons were sent to Brussels, and three years later seven of the tapestries were completed and displayed in Rome. They were an immense success and caused

a revolution of sorts in the art. In Raphael's design, the narrow border found in medieval tapestry was widened to form what was more or less a frame for the picture it contained. Filled with sometimes grotesque motifs, the frame itself became an important part of the composition. Tapestries had been based on paintings before: *The Virgin in Glory* in the Louvre, for example, completed in 1485, is a close copy of the painted model —including the frame—but never before had painters had such an influence upon weavers as they did now.

The Renaissance brought other changes. The Middle Ages had produced tapestry that reflected contemporary life. The figures, though romanticized to some degree and flattened like pictures on a playing card, were nonetheless basically of their own time and place. But with the Renaissance, tapestry switched to scenes from Greek and Roman mythology, and gods and nymphs moved over the warp in a new three-dimensional space.

*N*ow, too, there were commissions from noblemen who wished their battles or hunts to be enshrined. Take, for example, the series entitled the *Hunts of the Emperor Maximilian*, now hanging in the Louvre. These panels illustrate how noblemen hunted in each month of the year. The tapestries have depth; the range of color is wide; and the technique of the weavers reflects developments in contemporary art. The ripples and refractions of water in a pond, the striding shadows of riders and hounds, all are superbly conveyed by the same process of shading and hatching invented by the Coptic weavers of Egypt centuries before.

In the *Hunts of the Emperor Maximilian* and other hunting series, some of the virtues of medieval tapestry are retained and refined. Tapestry of the Middle Ages had amalgamated aspects of reality and art, bringing both contemporary scenes and the

TEXT CONTINUED ON PAGE 31

21

Tapestries for Our Time

GALERIE ALICE PAULI, LAUSANNE

Magdalena Abakanowicz

LEONARDO BEZZOLA

Elsi Giauque

BOB WESTERLAGE

Sheila Hicks

Once tapestries brought warmth to drafty medieval halls. Today they bring a different kind of warmth to the stark walls and sheer glass façades of modern architecture. All over the world architects and designers rely on wall hangings to add color, drama, and scale to interior space. The best of modern tapestries are, however, more than mere decorative complements to architecture; each of the hangings in the portfolio beginning on the opposite page stands alone as a work of abstract art. In fact, because many tapestries do not hang against a wall at all but are intended to be viewed from all sides, some critics think of them as a kind of soft sculpture. There is another significant difference: where woven fabric once told a story, now the fabric itself is the tapestry's content. Artists use materials ranging from naturally dyed wool, similar to that used by medieval weavers, to hanks of polyester and thick hemp cords. Whatever the medium, however, the new work is linked to tapestry of the past by the sensuous appeal of fiber and the unlimited variety of woven textures.

1. Startling as a staring Cyclops head, Abakan Rouge *is a shaped tapestry woven of sisal in 1969 by Magdalena Abakanowicz. By doing away with a rectangular format, and by creating whole environments with her three-dimensional hangings, Abakanowicz has moved the art of tapestry far beyond its traditional limitations.*

2. Made of silk and synthetic yarns precisely wrapped and woven on metal frames, Pure Spatial Element *is a hanging construction that the viewer can walk around and step into. It was made in 1968–69 by Elsi Giauque, a Swiss artist who is now in her seventies.*

3. Sheila Hicks, an innovative American artist who has worked with native weavers in such far-flung places as Morocco and southern India, produced this hanging in her own Paris atelier and exhibited it at the Grand Palais in 1972. It is made of linen fibers wrapped in silk; its romantic title translates as "I knew that if I visited you one day, I would end by passing my nights, too."

4. Hung from the branches of an oak tree for this photograph, Interlaced Tree Form, *a series of tubular shapes, knitted rather than woven, was made by Ted Hallman, who works and teaches in California.*

5. To obtain a variety of textures, the Catalan artist Joseph Grau-Garriga combines slit tapestry, wrapped fibers, and knotted tufts, which he shapes with scissors. His ironically titled Tapis Pobre *(Poor Tapestry) is a rich mélange of rugged materials.*

6. Wojciech Sadley, another artist from the renowned school of Polish weavers, makes truly pendulous hangings from various somber-colored fibers, some woven, some not. In this piece, knotted pile hangs down in hairy profusion from a tapestry-woven ground.

TED HALLMAN

Ted Hallman

ARRAS GALLERY, NEW YORK

Joseph Grau-Garriga

EMANUELA LEWANDOWSKA

Wojciech Sadley

1. ABAKANOWICZ, *Abakan Rouge*

2. GIAUQUE, *Pure Spatial Element*

3. Hicks, *Je savais que si j'y venais un jour, j'y passerais mes nuits*

4. HALLMAN, *Interlaced Tree Form*

5. GRAU-GARRIGA. *Tapis Pobre*

conventions of romantic and religious literature within the frame of the loom. The *Hunts of the Emperor* does this too, but in a more sophisticated way. The expressionless masks of medieval tapestry characters, derived from the impressive tapestries of the Copts and Byzantines, are gone. The faces of the huntsmen express triumph, fury, disappointment; those of the servants and varlets, trickiness, servility, hatred, amusement. In its own way, the series is a minor social commentary on the times, and there are touches of the humor of the times as well. In one of the panels, a dog obviously suffering from acute diarrhea appears in the foreground, its posterior presented to viewers, who could have included the emperor Charles V, who probably commissioned it.

Charles V was, in fact, very keen on tapestry, and from 1528 on raised the shield of his protection over the Flemish weavers. About ten years later the French king, Francis I, went one better and created at Fontainebleau his own tapestry manufactory, administered by the superintendent of royal buildings. By the end of the sixteenth century, tapestry collections had become a mania with the French. Foreign exchange was lavishly spent on Flemish tapestries and, since the Spaniards then held Flanders, this meant a considerable addition to the exchequers of Spain. Henry IV of France saw danger ahead. He forbade the import of tapestry, with the result that weavers from Flanders began to arrive in France in large numbers.

The inducements were tremendous. The weavers who arrived in France were accorded high social status, furnished with homes, and exempted from all taxes and levies. The sketches for the tapestries were made by the king's painters, and from 1600 to 1640 the output of the Parisian workshops was tremendous. (James I of England, driven to emulation, set up a tapestry manufactory at Mortlake near London in 1619.) In 1667 Colbert, finance minister to Louis XIV, declared that the health of a society was manifested by the state of its arts. He also felt that the main purpose of the arts was to laud the reigning king, and to this end he set up the Gobelins manufactory in Paris. It produced furnishings and decorations for the royal palaces and became the most famous factory in the history of tapestry.

The Gobelins manufactory was headed by Charles Le Brun, himself a painter. Le Brun established three workshops for vertical looms and two for horizontal looms, and all were plied by famous weavers. A staff of technicians told him of the special qualities of wool for tapestries, how it would behave in the light, what colors it would take best, and what it could and could not achieve pictorially. A staff of dyers, headed by a Flemish expert, had seventy-nine colors at their disposal. Of the eight hundred people who worked at the Gobelins manufactory around 1675, about sixty were painters. During his twenty-seven years at the head of the manufactory, Le Brun himself was responsible for the composition and execution of eight hundred and twenty-four large tapestries.

At the end of the seventeenth century, with the deaths of Colbert and Le Brun, new, more economical policies were instituted at the Gobelins factory: the weaving of Le Brun's series,

The Story of the King, was suspended and copies of sixteenth-century Flemish tapestries were begun. The switch back to Flemish influences meant that tapestry became more decorative, and mythological themes, which had been treated rather less seriously, returned to fashion. This trend had an influence on the way tapestry was used: as it became more decorative, it began to appear as upholstery for the chairs and sofas of boudoirs, for curtains, and for carpets. Tapestry continued to be popular for nearly a century. Then came the French Revolution in 1789 and an art that had always been exclusively for the rich began to decline in favor.

*A*cross the Seine from our hotel was the Louvre, impressive, and a little dead, rather like de Gaulle when he was alive. My wife and I walked over one of the bridges that lead to it, and I asked for the tapestry section. None of the attendants we spoke to seemed to know where it was, but eventually, climbing an obscure stairway, we reached the high-ceilinged room where the *Hunts of the Emperor Maximilian* hangs. We strolled around and looked the panels over, appreciating the reality of solid warp and woof: spring, and a swain caressing his girl in the bushes; winter, and the cobwebby nudity of the trees; the dead deer, the live people—and my friend, the defecating dog. After that we went through what used to be the state apartments, huge, solid rooms hung and upholstered in tapestries from the Gobelins factories. The upholstery was simply decorative, but the hangings on the walls depicted naval, military, and religious scenes.

Nobody lives like that any more, and tapestries these days are neither purely decorative nor devoted to historical or religious narratives. The Aubusson manufactory began in 1932 to make tapestries reproducing the work of French painters of the time, Picasso, Rouault, Braque, Dufy; and later, the artist Jean Lurçat produced his own cartoons and worked directly with the Aubusson weavers. Artists today who make tapestry often use methods quite different from classical techniques. These artist-weavers—concerned with the expressive possibilities of fiber, be it wool, hemp, or polyester—are making hangings that can no longer be called "pure" tapestry, but rather a form of environmental art.

We came out of the Louvre into a Parisian April smelling of dust, benzine, flowers, garlic, and French people. There were no unicorns in Paris that day, and not too many ladies. Though dogs still fouled the pavements, no serfs with low brows and curled smiles under their caps held them leashed. No prancing horses laden with lords in the vicinity. An art that has lost its subject matter has to die. Perhaps the place for tapestry now is behind the tall walls of museums, or in the rooms of gentle skeptics in universities.

At Oxford, where he learned about tapestry, Dom Moraes won the Hawthornden Poetry Prize. He has since published four books of verse and five others, including, last year, A Matter of People.

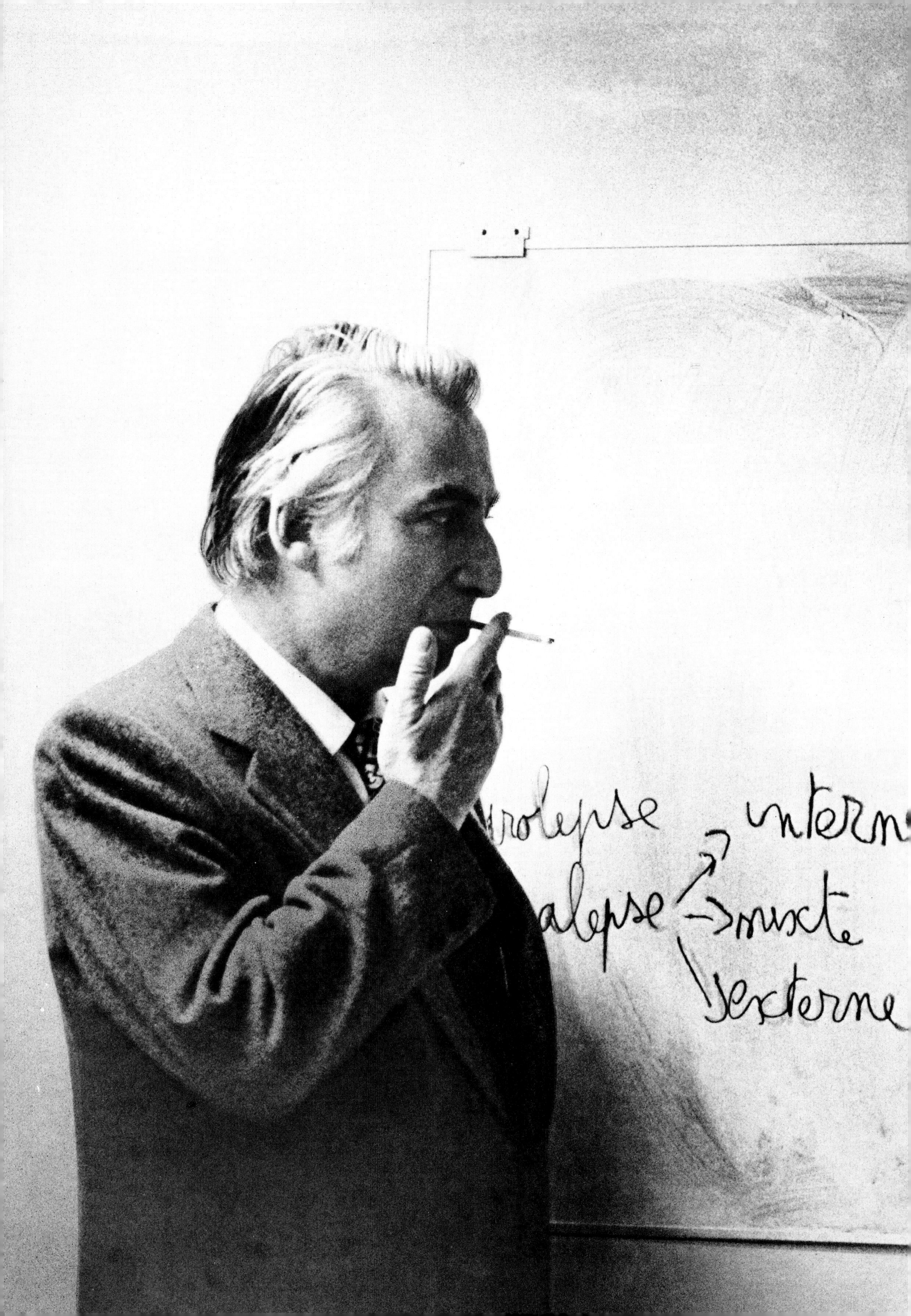
rolepse
intern
alepse
mixte
externe

"The Rear Guard of the Avant-Garde"

With righteous indignation, structuralism,
and something called semiotics, a multifaceted Frenchman
named Roland Barthes is capturing
a growing audience for his social and literary criticism

Does pop culture make you morose? Have you stopped smiling at television commercials? Do you have the suspicion that we are all getting more and more phony? On the positive side, are you trendy enough to be fascinated by linguistics? If so, you qualify as a member of the growing public for the social and literary criticism of Roland Barthes.

It is not that Barthes (pronounced "bart") is exactly a recent discovery. He has had a high, if controversial, reputation among intellectuals in his native France since the mid-1950's, plus a good deal of praise from up-to-date mandarins abroad. What is new and rather surprising is the sudden expansion of his fame after nearly two decades. His *Mythologies* and *Essais critiques,* which first appeared in France in 1957 and 1964 respectively, have recently been published in the United States, making a total of five of his books now available in English. During the past few years his work has also been translated into German, Italian, Spanish, Dutch, Norwegian, Swedish, Rumanian, Polish, Czech, Serbo-Croatian, and Japanese.

The Paris literary magazine *Tel Quel* ("Such as It Is"), which favors Maoist thought and experimental fiction, has devoted almost an entire issue to him; and so has the review *L'Arc,* which prefers avant-garde interdisciplinary

Barthes, opposite, contemplates linguistic mysteries at the Ecole Practique des Hautes Etudes in Paris, where he conducts seminars.

studies. The less far-out *New York Times* has hailed him as the creator of "a world of pure light and coherence." In sum, his elegant debunking, unabashed elitism, and dry cerebration seem to be filling a spreading need in the 1970's, possibly as antidotes for the hokum and bland egalitarianism of the 1960's.

This is not to say that Barthes is likely to flower into a chic cult hero and a French tourist attraction. He is a reserved, fifty-nine-year-old bachelor who looks like a deposed Bourbon monarch, sticks mostly to his Paris apartment behind the Church of Saint Sulpice, and would undoubtedly be acutely embarrassed by the role of gawked-at star talker in a Left Bank café. Lacking a doctorate and handicapped by the loss of the six years he spent as a patient in tuberculosis sanatoriums in France and Switzerland, he has improvised a respectable if unspectacular academic career: he conducts seminars at the Ecole Pratique des Hautes Etudes, a Paris institution that stresses science rather than literature.

Barthes' writings do not provide the sort of gospel that might fire a cultist imagination: the philosophical premises are unobtrusive, and the political attitudes, while revolutionary, are hard to reduce to slogans. His critical method is a mixture of semiotics, structuralism, Marxism, existentialism, Freudianism, and righteous indignation. He has modestly referred to himself as somebody occupying a position in "the rear guard of the avant-garde."

In other words, he resists being labeled. He might be described as a new-fashioned version of the old-fashioned French moralist, in a line that can be traced back to the satirists and rhetoricians of Roman antiquity. More simply, he can be called an unusually attentive reader, for he reads not only words but also the other signs by which a personality, class, or society may express itself—or give itself away.

The appropriate introduction to Barthes' work is his first book, *Le Degré zéro de l'écriture,* which was published in 1953 and whose title has been translated somewhat ambiguously as *Writing Degree Zero.* By *écriture* Barthes means not just "writing" but a recognizable kind of prose, something I would call a "style" if he did not prefer to reserve that term for personal style. The classical prose of Voltaire, with its emphasis on order and clarity, its air of being transparent, is an *écriture.* So is the prose of the typical mid-nineteenth-century French novel, with its predilection for the use of the third person and for verbs in the simple past, a tense almost never used in spoken French. So, too, is the stereotyped prose of many Communists, with judgments presented as facts and special meanings for words like "peace" and "democracy."

As these examples suggest, an *écriture* is for Barthes a manifestation of an ideology and to some extent a form of double talk. To adopt the *écriture classique* is to commit oneself, intentionally or not, to notions about com-

By ROY McMULLEN

mon reason and the universal nature of man that reflect the bourgeois ideology that began rising to power in the late seventeenth century. To adopt the *écriture* of the traditional French novel, which is also that of straight historical narrative, is to commit oneself to notions of fate and causality that falsify, at least in the modern existentialist view, the reality of choice in human life. To adopt the Communist *écriture* is to . . . but there is no need to belabor the point. No *écriture* is innocent.

Beset by the many *écritures* available, how can a writer be honest? How can he dodge the implicit commitments? How can he avoid being alienated? Attempts to answer these questions constitute a major part of the history of modern prose. Some writers, one of the first being Flaubert, have tried what Barthes calls the "artisan" approach and have sweated over their *mots justes*. Others have tortured and nearly murdered the language in their effort to get closer to reality. Some have retreated into a supposedly meaningful silence. And still others have sought to escape from dishonest "literature" by writing in an argot, a dialect, or some other sort of primarily oral language. Especially interesting to Barthes are those who, like Camus in *L'Etranger,* have tried to invent a neutral, colorless, purely instrumental, absolutely cold prose—have tried, that is, to get down to *le degré zéro de l'écriture*. The trouble, of course, is that each act of defiance has tended to become in its turn a convention and, finally, one more ideological subterfuge, for the modern bourgeoisie is notoriously capable of transforming censure into praise and co-opting opponents. Barthes concludes, a bit dispiritedly, that modern prose can be only an anticipation and that there can be no complete solution to the problem of "decorative and compromising" *écritures* without a social revolution. Double talk is the natural language of an ethically flawed society.

After the density of *Le Degré zéro de l'écriture,* the short, witty essays collected in *Mythologies* may seem to be

---

Fringe Benefits

In Joseph L. Mankiewicz's *Julius Caesar* [1953], all the characters are wearing fringes. Some have them curly, some straggly, some tufted, some oily, all have them well combed, and the bald are not admitted, although there are plenty to be found in Roman history. Those who have little hair have not been let off for all that, and the hairdresser—the king-pin of the film—has still managed to produce one last lock which duly reaches the top of the forehead, one of those Roman foreheads, whose smallness has at all times indicated a specific mixture of self-righteousness, virtue and conquest.

What then is associated with these insistent fringes? Quite simply the label of Roman-ness. We therefore see here the mainspring of the Spectacle—the *sign*—operating in the open. The frontal lock overwhelms one with evidence, no one can doubt that he is in Ancient Rome. And this certainty is permanent: the actors speak, act, torment themselves, debate "questions of universal import," without losing, thanks to this little flag displayed on their foreheads, any of their historical plausibility. Their general representativeness can even expand in complete safety, cross the ocean and the centuries, and merge into the Yankee mugs of Hollywood extras: no matter, everyone is reassured, installed in the quiet certainty of a universe without duplicity, where Romans are Romans thanks to the most legible of signs: hair on the forehead.

—*From* MYTHOLOGIES, 1957

---

only light entertainment. They were written between 1954 and 1956 in response to occasional inspirations, and are concerned with such matters as Garbo's face, wrestling matches, detergents, plastics, Martians and flying saucers, wine and milk, steaks and French fries, Charlie Chaplin, Billy Graham, stripteasers, astrology, and the politics of shopkeepers. There are bright thoughts in the aphoristic *écriture* of the French seventeenth century (Barthes has done a study of the maxims of La Rochefoucauld). A discussion of a magazine sob sister's advice to the lovelorn

opens with fine sententiousness: "The heart is a female organ." In an account of a guidebook we are given a law of the genre: "Christianity is the leading provisioner in tourism; one travels only to visit churches." An essay on a child prodigy yields: "In the time of Pascal childhood was considered a lost period; the problem was to get out of it as soon as possible. Since the Romantic era (since the triumph, that is, of the bourgeoisie) the problem is to stay in it as long as possible."

There is entertainment, too, in his habit of explaining presumably ignoble art in terms of the noble. Having observed that a professional wrestler exaggerates his plight when pinned down, Barthes adds: "The gesture of the vanquished wrestler signaling to the world a defeat which, far from concealing, he accentuates and *holds* in the fashion of a fermata in music, corresponds to the ancient mask that was designed to signify the tragic tone. . . ."

These essays are not, however, just deadpan divertissements and cultural slumming; they are also protests, like *Le Degré zéro de l'écriture,* against the humbug in our society. The piece on the advice to the lovelorn column becomes a denunciation of the way women's magazines, "amid trumpet blasts about Feminine Independence," convert their readers into "a colony of parasites" dependent on men and wretchedly isolated from the real world. The piece on the guidebook criticizes the kind of tourism that reduces a country to a museum. A review of the photographic exhibition *The Family of Man* condemns the sentimentality that stresses our common human lot—birth, work, death—and thus diverts attention from the unjust differences. Sometimes Barthes is ironical to the point of approval: he obviously likes the play-acting of wrestlers, probably because in this instance the myth fools nobody. But he is relentless against the alibis of the well-off, the paltering of admen, the dream-mongering of the popular press, and every sort of modern tartuffe.

His Marxism and his existentialism

appear in *Mythologies* in the form of attacks on "the bourgeois norm" and on the complacent tacit assumption, which he ties to philosophical essentialism, that our spuriousness and silliness are somehow built-in instead of being produced by historical circumstances that can be controlled—if need be, by a violent political revolt. "I was trying," he explains in his foreword, "to reflect regularly on certain myths in French daily life . . . . The point of departure for this reflection was most often a feeling of impatience when confronted by the 'naturalness' with which the press, art, and common sense constantly dress up a reality which, even though it is the one we live in, is nevertheless completely historical; in brief, it pained me to see Nature and History confused at every turn in accounts of our daily behavior, and I wanted, in this decked-out display of what-goes-without-saying, to get hold of the ideological abuse which in my opinion is hidden there." Toward the end of the book he returns to this theme, insisting that what is called human nature in a capitalist society is mostly just a set of customs that are convenient and profitable for the dominant class.

In all this there is an evident implication that a myth, in the special sense under scrutiny, is a piece of ideological double talk comparable to an *écriture,* with allowances for the frequent use of images or actions or other substitutes for words. A concluding chapter, entitled "Myth Today," renders the linguistic analogy explicit. Here Barthes makes his first detailed venture into semiotics, the general theory of signs and symbols; and the result, while often heavy going, is the elaboration of a theoretical structure that has the merit of being applicable to many matters besides those evoked in *Mythologies.*

Briefly, the idea is that a "myth" is a semiotic operation on two interlocking levels. On the first level, which is that of all ordinary language operations, there are three elements: the "signifier," the "signified," and the sense that emerges from the signifier-signified relationship, which Barthes confusingly chooses to call the "sign." (It must be remembered that semiotics is a young science with a terminology that is mostly a mess.) On the second level, which is where mythicizing occurs, there are again three elements, but here the "sign," or sense, that emerged on the first level is converted into a "signifier" and used to generate a new sense—one, two, three on the first level, and then presto, three, four, five on the second level. To put the matter more crudely, the mythmaker is both a misappropriator of signs and a semiotical con man who steals a meaning and uses it to say something else.

Barthes draws one case from a magazine he once saw in a Paris barbershop, apparently around the beginning of the Algerian War: "On the cover a young Negro dressed in a French uniform is saluting, his eyes raised and fixed without doubt on the folds of the tricolored flag. That is the *sense* of the image. But, naive or not, I see very well what the image signifies— that France is a great Empire, that all her sons, without distinction of color, serve faithfully under her flag, and that there is no better answer to the disparagers of an alleged colonialism than the zeal of this black man in the service of his alleged oppressors."

Here the advantages, for the mythmaker, of the two semiotic levels are evident. The picture of the young Negro is not in itself a symbol of French imperialism, nor in any way a stimulator of bogus sentiment; in fact, it is an image that on the first level is rich, fresh, and utterly blameless. And so, when misappropriated for the second level, it may seduce an unwary viewer in a fashion beyond the capacity of an imperial symbol or straight propaganda.

An American should have no difficulty in finding similar examples of mythmaking in more recent history. Both the Vietnam War and the Watergate affair teemed with them, and both involved lavish use of a favorite White House first-semiotic-level ma-neuver: an expression of concern, in itself perfectly legitimate, over national security. (Both also, incidentally, saw the blooming of some highly "decorative and compromising" *écritures.*)

Governments bent on dubious adventures are not, of course, the only offenders, nor the most important. Madison Avenue has been working on the two semiotic levels long enough to do it sometimes just for laughs, like an actor spoofing a role he has played too often. Militant conservatives have their law-and-order brand of obscurantism. Militant leftists have had their Soviet tractor girls and now have their smiling Chinese and their sloe-eyed Plains Indians. Freedom from censorship translates into sex shops.

Obviously, all noble-minded activities, precisely because they *are* in themselves noble-minded, offer excellent structures for mythmaking in the Barthesian sense. Every earnest town planner is dauntingly familiar with the fact that "urban renewal" on the first semiotic level frequently signifies, on the second level, "get the blacks out," and every environmentalist is aware of how easily the term "clean air" can come to mean, "you're a stinker if you don't buy our system of emission reduction."

A great deal of the fiercest criticism in *Mythologies,* however, is directed against the myths that are not so much concocted as secreted—to some extent by all of us, although perhaps most insistently by the lower middle class (the silent majority) and its leaders. These myths are characterized by a number of ugly little fooling devices that function as "rhetorical figures" in the semiotic system. One such is "vaccination," the familiar trick, much prized by "liberal" reactionaries, of admitting a small evil in order to ignore a large one.

Another, more subtle, device is "identification," the refusal to grant the integral difference of other people; this can have the convenient effect, for example, of making black or poor people and their specific problems practically invisible to an affluent white man. Still another "figure" is the flat tautology:

"A is A and B is B because that's how things are." Another is the "neither-nor" locution that balances issues in order to get rid of them. All these devices can seem to reflect proverbial wisdom, and are thus examples of the fake "naturalness," the "display of what-goes-without-saying," that often hides "ideological abuse."

In 1964 Barthes developed his ideas about semiotics in a short treatise translated as *The Elements of Semiology*. In 1967, after working on the project for nearly ten years, he published *Système de la Mode,* a study of the "language" of women's fashions. Although both these books are worth reading for definitions and insights, neither is wholly successful. *Eléments de sémiologie* is marred by a lack of familiarity with the work of American linguists of the Chomsky generation. *Système de la Mode* suffers from being focused not on clothes directly but on what fashion writers say about clothes; and I have a feeling that the author himself, during his long labor, finally became weary of the contrast between his massive analytical apparatus and his ephemeral data.

In the meantime he was steadily turning out essays on literature, some of which were collected in 1963 in *Sur Racine* and in 1964 in *Essais critiques.* To these volumes, and the mysteriously titled *S/Z* of 1970, now available in English, a reader of French should add the *Sade, Fourier, Loyola* of 1971, and the *Nouveaux essais critiques* included in a 1972 Paris pocketbook edition of *Le Degré zéro de l'écriture.* The first thing that strikes the reader is the wide range of Barthes' interests. In addition to the major studies of Racine, Sade, Fourier, and Loyola, there are pieces on such contemporary innovators as Alain Robbe-Grillet and Michel Butor; on the historian Michelet; on Proust, Pierre Loti, Flaubert, Balzac, Baudelaire, Chateaubriand, Voltaire, La Bruyère, and La Rochefoucauld; on Kafka and Brecht; on Tacitus and Aeschylus.

Running through the various essays, however, are certain recurring approaches that pull everything together

Unspeaking the Unspeakable

I read the text. This statement, consonant with the "genius" of the language (subject, verb, complement), is not always true. The more plural the text, the less it is written before I read it; I do not make it undergo a predicative operation, consequent upon its being, an operation known as *reading*, and *I* is not an innocent subject, anterior to the text, one which will subsequently deal with the text as it would an object to dismantle or a site to occupy. This "I" which approaches the text is already itself a plurality of other texts, of codes which are infinite or, more precisely, lost (whose origin is lost). *Objectivity* and *subjectivity* are of course forces which can take over the text, but they are forces which have no affinity with it. Subjectivity is a plenary image, with which I may be thought to encumber the text, but whose deceptive plenitude is merely the wake of all the codes which constitute me, so that my subjectivity has ultimately the generality of stereotypes. Objectivity is the same type of replenishment: it is an imaginary system like the rest (except that here the castrating gesture is more fiercely characterized), an image which serves to name me advantageously, to make myself known, "misknown," even to myself. Reading involves risks of objectivity or subjectivity (both are imaginary) only insofar as we define the text as an expressive object (presented for our own expression), sublimated under a morality of truth, in one instance laxist; in the other, ascetic.

—*From* s/z, 1970

and explain why Barthes is known in France as the leading representative of the postwar *nouvelle critique.* This literary movement, although not at all organized, is coherent enough to be described as an updated French version of the New Criticism that arose in England and America between the world wars. Like its foreign predecessor, *la nouvelle critique* stresses the use of nonliterary disciplines (the social sciences, for instance) in the study of literature, insists on the necessity of a close reading of the text, often prefers to consider a work as isolated from the context

of its creation, and at times unearths levels of supposed significance that can disconcert a plain man who assumes that words mean what they say.

In *Sur Racine,* for example, Barthes reduces the tragic Racinean universe and its population to a structuralist, existentialist, and Freudian mechanism that churns out systematic oppositions —shade-light, silence-language, virility-femininity, authority-submission—and throbs with oedipal conflict. He adds to this analytical tour de force a flat, provocative statement that he is making "no reference" whatever to possible biographical and historical sources for Racine's work.

In *S/Z* he pushes a thematic and semiotical study of a Balzac novelette, *Sarrasine,* into a network of plural meanings unexpected enough to be called, by his own cheerful admission, a "rewrite" of the original text. The story concerns the unfortunate love of a duped eighteenth-century French sculptor, Sarrasine, for a beautiful Italian soprano, Zambinella, who turns out to be a *castrato* dressed as a woman. The title of the critical essay, Barthes explains, separates the initials of these personages with a diagonal because "S" and "Z" are the same letter, or at least mirror images; because in Zambinella Sarrasine contemplates his own unmanning; and because the diagonal is used by linguists to mean "versus."

Naturally, this sort of criticism has irritated French literary scholars, in particular those who like to trace sources and influences on a writer's work. They have accused Barthes of discrediting national institutions, ignoring common sense, playing fast and loose with facts, employing jargon, yielding to sexual obsessions, giving classics a modern ideological slant, and treating language as something halfway between molasses and rubber. One of the most effective detractors has been Raymond Picard, a Sorbonne professor, an expert on Racine, and the author of a long pamphlet entitled *Nouvelle critique ou nouvelle imposture?* The new French critic, he remarks, is like "a man who might be interested in women but who, by a strange perversion, can appreciate them only by examining them with X rays."

Barthes has answered his adversaries partly by accusing them of concealing their own ideological commitments under a pretense of objectivity, and partly by maintaining that one must get inside a literary production in order to understand it and judge it properly. Does this requirement involve a risk of complete subjectivity, of total confusion between the roles of critic and creator? If so, Barthes doesn't mind; in an interview he has said, "Let's say that in the transitional state of today's writing the roles are blurred without being abolished. For my part, I do not consider myself a critic, but a novelist, a scribe."

You do not have to be a Sorbonne professor, of course, to find this remark, coming from a professional critic, a little short on seriousness. Nor do you have to be a hopeless reactionary to find other reasons for being frequently irked by Barthes. His harping attacks on the wicked representatives of the bourgeoisie can be tiresome, largely because he is so vague about identifying these scoundrels that he leaves you with the suspicion that, like Sartre's hell, they are just "the others," the non-Barthesian people. His puncturing of "myths" can imply, in a rather uncomplimentary fashion, that he assumes you were taken in before he came along. His addiction to semiotics can turn into scientism. (He has admitted that at one point in his career he "traversed a euphoric dream of scientific-ness.") His neologisms, puns, asides, and Jamesian syntax made him a latter-day *précieux* (although not *ridicule*). But long before your complaints become a final exasperation, you are likely to be appeased by his intelligence and also by his pure enthusiasm for signs and language as such. This is central in two of Barthes' more recent books, *L'empire des signes* (1970) and *Le plaisir du texte* (1973).

The "empire of signs" is Japan, which Barthes visited as a tourist intent on enjoying signifiers different from those in bourgeois France: "Why Japan? Because it is the land of writing. Of all the countries the author has had a chance to know, Japan is the one in which he has encountered the sign-work the closest to his convictions and his phantasms, or, if you like, the furthest from the loathing, irritation, and refusal stirred up in him by the Occidental semiocracy." He found "writing" of superb quality not only in the art of calligraphy but nearly everywhere: in painting, interior decoration, rock-and-sand gardens, actors' made-up faces, traditional manners, chopsticks, even the student riots.

Whit struck him was the gratuitousness, the sheer "emptiness" of these "writings." To be sure, in the national script this peculiar emptiness was partly an effect of his ignorance of the language. But the same odd absence of meaning was pervasive. The haiku, he discovered in a flash of illumination, was not the lesson in conciseness it has often been called; it was simply a lovely example of insignificance. The deep bows and the other elements in the complex ritual of Japanese courtesy were an "exercise in the void," a rite unencumbered by Western respect for the individual personality. The flowerless gardens, he noted, had really no message at all to deliver. Immersed in marvelous signifiers that were all the more marvelous because they signified virtually nothing, he experienced a sudden, gratifying, "in no way solemn" blank—the equivalent of a Zen satori.

This almost mystical pleasure in semiotics minus semantics may seem a long way from the irreverence, the structural analysis, the semantic alertness, and the moralizing in *Mythologies*. But there is, of course, a connecting thread. It can be argued that only a person who is sensitive to signifiers as signifiers is likely to see through a modern mythmaker, for in fact the latter, in his own iniquitous way, is a connoisseur of media as such. The sly meaning, or insinuation, in a myth arises not so much from a "content"—the young Negro

saluting, for instance—as from an illicit manipulation of a "content" as a mere signifier. In a sense, you have to "empty" the apparatus in order to perceive how it works, and if you don't "empty" it you are almost certain to be hooked by it. Hence, there is only a seeming paradox in saying that Barthes would not be the ardent moralist he is if he were not also an ardent formalist.

In *Le plaisir du texte* he is back in France, engaged again in his favorite occupation, reading. The book is extremely laconic, even gnomic, in style, perhaps because, as he remarks, "the distinctive characteristic of enjoyment is unspeakableness." As in all his works, there are unfamiliar terms for familiar things, and familiar terms used in unfamiliar ways; he is an indefatigable and generally stimulating namer. But for ordinary consumers of literature the best passages are those in which he lingers over "the pleasure of the text."

Barthes grants that a traditional novel can be read rapidly and agreeably just for the sake of the plot, the bare story: ". . . we skip with impunity (nobody sees us) the descriptions, the explanations, the considerations, the conversations; we are like spectators in a cabaret who would like to climb up on the stage and hasten the strip-tease." He maintains, however, that a properly modern text demands a leisurely, "aristocratic" manner of perusal; it has to be "nibbled at, not gulped," or else it becomes "opaque, barred to your pleasure."

The severe description Barthes gives of such a modern "text for enjoyment" fits very well the kind of text he himself has been producing during the past twenty years: "[It] discomforts (perhaps to the point of boring) the reader, shakes his historical, cultural, and psychological foundations, unsettles the consistency of his tastes, his values, and his memories, and provokes a crisis in his relations with language."

Roy McMullen is fascinated by twentieth-century French intellectuals. See the Autumn, 1969, HORIZON for his article about the philosopher Michel Foucault.

Six Crises in Cookery

From a mess of pottage to chicken Marengo,
here are great moments in culinary history, selected by an artist and re-created in savory detail

A BOUQUET GARNI OF ETCHINGS FOR HORIZON BY ZEVI BLUM

Food need not be a mere necessity of life. Some use it as the occasion for an intricately choreographed production number. Consider, for example, the diners above. They are enjoying the hospitality of a rich Roman merchant, Apicius, the reputed first-century A.D. author of what may be the oldest compendium of recipes, *De Re Coquinaria,* or *The Art of Cooking.* Like all properly planned Roman banquets, this one was divided into two parts — the first devoted primarily to eating, the second to drinking. Guests were limited to no more than nine, not counting dancing girls and courtesans (the only women invited). Among the delicacies he offered, Apicius no doubt served the rich stews, sauces, and cakes for which he was famous (one author notes sourly that "the strongest passion of this gourmandizing fool was for ragouts of half-a-hundred more or less incongruous elements"). Apicius had good reason for making this banquet a lavish one: it was to be his last. Discovering that he had spent a hundred million sesterces on food and drink over the years, and having a mere ten thousand left, he decided to end his life rather than face a banquetless future. Down through the ages, there have been many other great moments in cookery — though few of them quite so final. Here are a half-dozen of our favorites, as interpreted by that fiendishly imaginative artist, Zevi Blum.　　　—K. E.

Chicken Leg ...

*I*t was Napoleon, above, who reputedly remarked that an army marches on its stomach. Whatever can be said of other armies, his certainly did, even to the extent of making that notable contribution to cookery, *poulet sauté à la Marengo*. Legend has it that during the entire day of June 14, 1800, while fighting the Austrians at Marengo, Napoleon had eaten nothing. Suddenly hungry, he ordered his chef, Dunand, to prepare a meal. But provisions were scarce. Dunand sent his men to scour the Piedmontese countryside, where they found chickens, eggs, tomatoes, olive oil, garlic, bread, and, in a meandering stream, a few crayfish. The chef gently fried the chicken and eggs in the oil and garlic, added the tomatoes, water, and a little brandy, and steamed the crayfish along with the chicken. Delighted, Napoleon told Dunand, "You must feed me like this after every battle." Dunand, feeling that the crayfish were too unusual a garnish, once omitted them from the recipe. The emperor was not amused. "You have left out the crayfish," he complained. "It will bring me bad luck." The crayfish were promptly reinstated.

*T*o many Frenchmen, a meal without potatoes is no meal at all, yet the potato has been part of French cuisine for only two hundred years. Introduced into Europe in the 1540's, the lowly potato was long shunned by the French—some authorities even thought it caused leprosy. But Antoine Auguste Parmentier knew potatoes were not poisonous: captured by the Germans in 1761, he had lived on little else for more than a year. He began his campaign for the vegetable in 1771 by publishing a thesis that puffed the potato as a nutritious foodstuff during famines (other tempting morsels were iris bulbs and couch grass). In 1785, warming to his task, he presented Louis XVI with a small bouquet of potato flowers. Louis put one of the purplish blooms into his buttonhole, and the rage for the potato plant was on. Parmentier continued his publicizing. He served an elaborate dinner, including a "fish" course composed entirely of potatoes. And then, in 1787, he planted fifty acres on the Sablon plain in potatoes and, to excite curiosity, had the field closely watched during the day by the Garde Française, left. But every publicity campaign has its limits: at night, the soldiers went home, leaving the precious field unguarded. Fortunately for gastronomy, the potato plants survived.

For sheer pomp, circumstance, and calories, no era in the history of cookery surpasses the reign of Louis XIV. Whether dining alone or with his court, Louis ate often and well. The customary meal consisted of eight artfully orchestrated courses (the fish was served after the roasts "to remove the taste of the meat"). As each course became ready for serving, a grand procession formed, including stewards, musicians, gentlemen and ladies in waiting, and, lost somewhere in the midst of all this, the food itself, rapidly turning stone

cold. Courtiers of the time vied for the honor of feeding and amusing *le roi*. Louis II de Bourbon, best known as Le Grand Condé, is said to have once fêted the king with an elaborate banquet. The fish was a giant turbot, the biggest ever seen. As the procession wound its way into the dining room, the overburdened waiters bearing the giant fish tripped, and the turbot crashed to the floor. Unperturbed, the host declared, " 'Tis but a trifle. Bring in the other turbot." A second turbot was promptly borne in, just as large, just as magnificent. Dinner proceeded on schedule.

Unjust Desserts

*I*n the annals of cookery, even a simple mess of pottage can prove significant. Pottage, a hearty soup that is simple to make and satisfying to the appetite, is to this day a staple in Middle Eastern households, just as it was in biblical times. In the book of Genesis, Esau, a hunter, was the elder of twins sired by Isaac. His brother was named Jacob. One day Esau returned from the hunt to find Jacob preparing lentil soup. Exhausted and famished, Esau cried, "Feed me, I pray thee, with that same red pottage; for I am faint." Jacob, knowing that the bearded Esau was his father's favorite because of his love of hunting, replied that Esau must first make over his birthright to him. Esau's hunger overcame all else: "Behold, I am at the point to die: and what profit shall this birthright do to me?" He swore to give up his birthright. Thus was biblical history made, for it was Jacob, not Esau, who became the progenitor of the twelve tribes of Israel.

*T*he chef's lot has often been a hard one. These days, should the rice burn or the soufflé collapse, there is always something in the freezer. Not so in times past. Jean François Vatel, the unfortunate maître d'hôtel opposite, came a cropper in April, 1671, when Louis XIV arrived at Le Grand Condé's château with a vast retinue. The first night, there wasn't enough roast meat; Vatel was mortified. Next morning, according to legend, he was told that the supply of fish was insufficient for that evening's repast. Declaring, "I cannot outlive this disgrace," Vatel retired to his room and succeeded, on the third try, in running his sword through his heart—at the precise moment more fish arrived. Although the *Larousse Gastronomique* takes Vatel severely to task ("he did not know how to make the best of a bad job"), the lesson is clear: if one's culinary skill is found wanting, one's world is indeed without hope.

INFLATION

By J. H. PLUMB

Economists pontificate; sociologists pontificate; politicians promise nostrums. Treasury officials work out the complex machinery of wage and price controls. Almost always to no avail. The debate goes on and on and on, and so does inflation.

Inflation is almost as complex as cancer, and about as curable. It can affect specific countries or areas and leave the rest of the world untouched. What happened in Brazil after World War II, and in Germany after World War I—where a man had to have a briefcase to carry enough marks to buy lunch—was more a local than an international phenomenon. The experience was chronic, devastating, yet specific. The rest of the world —economically speaking—was not greatly affected, although the social and political consequences of the German inflation were to prove catastrophic. However, inflation can also be widespread and long-term—an intermittent fever that crests sharply from time to time but never dies away, lasting, perhaps, for a century.

It was this variety of the disease that afflicted Europe between 1530 and 1620, a variety more like our present circumstances than the dramatic inflationary spiral of Weimar Germany or the temporary, if sharp, inflation in France and England during the Napoleonic Wars.

For more than a generation historians have been fascinated by the continuous inflation in sixteenth-century Europe and have probed deeply into its causes. They came up initially with the neat explanation that the trouble lay with a sudden increase in money supply. In the

sixteenth century Europe, via Spain, was flooded with bullion, firstly gold from the Aztecs and Incas, and then vast quantities of silver from the mines of Potosí. What further explanation was needed?

Alas, so simple a theory was soon disproved. A Scandinavian scholar, Ingrid Hammarström, demonstrated that inflation had hit the tiny communities of Sweden, which the bullion never reached, as hard as it hit Spain. The Aztec and Inca gold was of no fundamental consequence, and inflation was steaming ahead long before the

PHILIP II   LORD BURGHLEY   JAMES I

Despite the vast power they wielded, these three men had virtually no success in checking the disastrous inflation of their time.

mountain of silver at Potosí had been discovered. Thus, money supply was no answer, although most historians would agree that a sudden influx of huge quantities of bullion can send the temperature of inflation up a degree or two over a short period. As a fundamental cause, money supply was dropped; nevertheless, it remains a secondary contributory factor, helping to sustain rather than cause inflation.

What, then, does cause inflation? Almost certainly the growth of population, but growth in highly specialized circumstances. In the sixteenth century, as in our own time, the first and strongest in-

flationary pressure was on the cost of food, then clothing, then manufactured goods; indeed, food prices remained the basic problem. Nevertheless, rapid population growth has not always resulted in inflation—one need think only of Ireland in the first half of the nineteenth century. Only when the demand for food puts pressure on the capacity to meet that demand will prices rise, and the long-term pressure must be steady.

In so complex a situation as inflation, there are other factors besides. As trade and exchange grow more feverish, so the need for credit increases and interest rates rise, increasing the risks as they increase prices. The fever becomes so intense that society itself is endangered. But the causes of sixteenth-century inflation are of less interest to us than the consequences.

The consequences of sixteenth-century inflation were profound and long-lasting. At first, inflation acted as a catalyst, stimulating primary production of all kinds. The prudent, intelligent, up-to-date small farmer could do well, as could the intelligent, prudent, cautiously experimental landlord.

Trade was riskier, but it could, and did, bring vast fortunes to large-scale capitalists. They spread their risks in commodities so that they could ride out the gluts and exploit the shortages.

Inflation can, and does, make a few men very rich, either on a larger or a smaller scale. Hence there is always a powerful sector of society quite happy to let inflation run its course. Inflation, however, makes most men poor. In Elizabethan times the grain traders and monopolists who could force up prices were the targets of bitter denunciation. There was a growing distrust of the *nouveaux riches,* a steady intensification of bitterness that soured political life. Real wages, not only for laborers but also for craftsmen and artisans, fell steadily. Widespread poverty drove the poor into the towns and created a nightmare of anxiety for the Tudor government. Officials were forced into social and economic legislation of the most authoritarian and complex kind. Lord Burghley, Elizabeth's secretary of state, produced a wage-and-price policy with formidable statutory sanctions, but it had no effect. His poverty programs did little better. Indeed, one of the ironies of inflation is that it forces governments to attempt complex remedial measures that rarely have any effect except to intensify class bitterness on the one hand and distrust of government on the other.

One of the most fascinating consequences, however, of an inflationary world is the strong emotions it generates for material objects. Although it does promote competitive buying of intrinsically valuable goods, from houses to jewels, it also provokes a hatred of waste. Material possessions, therefore, are imbued with intense, yet complex, moral feeling. Certainly in sixteenth-century Europe there developed the attitude that ostentation was wicked, that riches could be dangerous to the soul. To put the matter bluntly, inflation helped foster a puritan attitude to riches that cut right across denominational religion. In Catholic France as in Protestant England, austerity was regarded as a virtue.

This same attitude exists in our own time, with its concern for recycling and protection of resources. There is also, today, at least among the middle class, an aversion to ostentatious dress that echoes the sobriety and plainness of the European middle class in the mid-seventeenth century. Our attack on waste— whether in packaging or large cars—is like the seventeenth-century attack on ostentatious living. We can, therefore, expect a movement toward austerity.

Within a decade, it may well seem sinful not to dress like a Chinese peasant.

If this were the only effect of inflation, the future would seem less dark; but there are others. The powerful reactions to inflation that took place in the seventeenth century are mirrored in what is happening in our own time. For example, it is probable that there will be a sharp decline in population growth (West Germany and the United States have already fallen below zero population increase). This may be excellent in the long run, but it will create chronic economic and social problems in the short run. Certainly, this is what happened in the seventeenth century.

However, the worst possible consequence of inflation has always been its corrosion of political institutions. Every monarchy in the sixteenth century except the English went bankrupt. War, grandiose ambitions, and civil and religious strife played their part, and acquired extra force because of inflation. The cost of government and of armies soared; traditional revenues could not keep pace; interest rates flew toward the sky, and bankruptcy followed for bankers as well as monarchs. No government was able to control the process. At their wits' end for money, governments sold honors—anyone could buy an earldom or a baronetcy from James I. Government offices were sold to the highest bidder. The sale of licenses for monopolies became commonplace, and prices rose again.

Almost every financial action taken by any government in the sixteenth and early seventeenth centuries led to social and political discontent. Ministers were hated, vilified, and used up with remarkable rapidity by monarchs who increasingly felt that all criticism was iniquitous. Representative assemblies, no matter how limited their social base, became anathema to kings and rapidly began to disappear. Even in England, Parliament had to wage war to maintain its privileges, and elsewhere parliaments vanished, replaced by absolute monarchs backed by increasingly efficient

bureaucracies. In an inflationary world the nostrum is always authority—the power to impose. And yet, Philip II of Spain, who had more direct power, perhaps, than any other monarch of his time, was as powerless to check inflation as Elizabeth I of England, who had to share some of her authority in finance with Parliament. Nevertheless, the mood among men of property and authority, then, as now, was that only a great increase of power at the center could check the rot that inflation was creating in the social fabric.

Few, I think, would deny that our own political system may also be put seriously at risk by inflation. Every politician, every party, has some cure to sell to the electorate. Mr. Wilson attempted to impose an income and prices policy, and was checked by the trade unions. Mr. Heath imposed a policy of legislation and was wrecked and defeated. Everybody promises solutions, but none of them works because the inflationary forces are not national. The intricate interlocking economies of the free world make isolation virtually impossible. So, as politicians' programs fail and their promises boomerang, a fickle electorate turns to fringe parties or extravagant remedies, with the inevitable result of weakening the central government, as in Italy and Great Britain. Weak central government makes even moderate control of inflationary forces improbable. And so politicians and political institutions fall further into disrepute, and the rage of society grows. Political institutions, no matter how venerable, crumble with surprising ease. Old ideologies disappear with equal alacrity. New and harsh social moods can spread with astonishing speed. Inflation acts like the Black Death on political values.

If the resonances from the past ring clear and undistorted, what is certain is that once inflation leaps beyond control everything is in danger—our attitudes to life, our institutions, and, above all, our political systems. The strain is always heaviest at the center. The tempests are beginning to blow, and they will rage for years to come.

HENRY MAYHEW'S
OTHER LONDON

The chimney sweeps, the streetwalkers, the little match girls,
the down-and-outers--these were the Londoners that a pioneering
journalist wove into a memorable document of social history

In a sunless thoroughfare, teeming with the street life of Victorian London, a policeman vainly tries to direct traffic.

Toward the end of *Oliver Twist*, Charles Dickens introduces his readers to "the filthiest, the strangest, the most extraordinary of the many localities that are hidden in London, wholly unknown even by name, to the great mass of its inhabitants."

To reach this place, the visitor has to penetrate through a maze of close, narrow, and muddy streets, thronged by the roughest and poorest of waterside people. . . . He makes his way with difficulty along, assailed by offensive sights and smells from the narrow alleys . . . he walks beneath tottering housefronts projecting over the pavement, dismantled walls that seem to totter as he passes, chimneys half crushed half hesitating to fall, windows guarded by rusty iron bars that time and dirt have almost eaten away, every imaginable sign of desolation and neglect.

This horrifying rookery was Jacob's Island, beyond Dockhead in Bermondsey, one of the most notorious of the riverside slums in early Victorian London. Approached by rickety wooden bridges over a slimy ditch, Jacob's Island was a noisome warren of decaying houses whose windows, windows no more, looked forlornly down upon "every repulsive lineament of poverty, every loathsome indication of filth, rot, and garbage" that lined the muddy banks of Folly Ditch.

Twelve years after *Oliver Twist* was published, "in the year one thousand eight hundred and fifty," as Dickens wrote in a preface to a new edition of his book, "it was publicly declared in London by an amazing Alderman, that Jacob's Island did not exist, and never had existed. Jacob's Island continues to exist (like an ill-bred place as it is)."

One of Dickens's readers did know the full and terrible reality of Jacob's Island, where the cholera epidemic that swept across London in 1832 had begun, and where, in 1848, cholera broke out again. This man was a fellow writer, Henry Mayhew.

Mayhew paid a visit to Jacob's Island in 1849 when the cholera epidemic was at its height. What he saw, and later described, makes Dickens's account seem almost discreet. Mayhew wrote of the disgusting graveyard smell of the place, the heavy bubbles rising in the slimy, green-black water choked with rotting weeds and fish heads, the swollen carcasses of dead animals ready to burst with the gasses of putrefaction, and the red effluent from leather dressers. He described what Dickens, with his concern for the susceptibilities of his public, would never have dared describe: the open, doorless privies, the dark streaks of filth running down the walls where the house drains emptied into the ditch.

As a result of his visit, Mayhew suggested to the editor of the *Morning Chronicle* a series of articles on that part of London life almost as foreign to the

Gregarious and witty in private life, Henry Mayhew appears unnaturally magisterial in this portrait. It and the engravings on the following pages appeared in the 1861-62 edition of London Labour and the London Poor.

well-to-do citizens of the West End and the genteel suburbs as life in China. And from those articles there eventually developed that sociological masterpiece, *London Labour and the London Poor*, a work that vividly reveals, amid a vast amount of detailed information and carefully tabulated statistics, the enduring realities of East End life, the day-to-day existence of the poor and the oppressed, their sorrows and hopes, the way they thought and talked, the appalling conditions in which so many of them passed their days and nights. It is "a picture of London life so wonderful, so awful, so piteous and pathetic, so exciting and terrible," wrote one contemporary critic, William Makepeace Thackeray, "that readers of romance own they never read anything like to it; and that the griefs, struggles, strange adventures here depicted exceed anything that any of us could imagine. Yes; and these wonders and terrors have been lying by your door and mine ever since we had a door of our own. We had but to go a hundred yards off and see, for ourselves, but we never did."

What kind of man was he, this journalist who so shocked and moved his generation? An engraving of Henry Mayhew depicts a solemn if rather quizzical-looking middle-aged man, with a long nose and heavy jowls, balding, soberly dressed—the kind of man one might expect to be capable of the hard work, patience, perseverance, and determination that the compilation of a large-scale sociological study must entail. But the real Henry Mayhew was cheerful, lively, witty, gregarious, improvident, and wayward—quite clearly a charming, irresponsible, and delightfully good-natured personality.

"He was a fascinating companion," wrote one old friend, "and a man of inexhaustible resource and humour—though humour was but one side of his brilliant mind. Indolence was his besetting sin." He was "an admirable all round talker," according to another friend, the engraver Henry Vizetelly. "He would talk like a book on any subject for hours together if he could only find listeners, but could with difficulty be brought to put pen to paper." Although he made "considerable sums by writing, he never seemed to have a shilling; and most of the letters he received were from dunning creditors."

He was passionately interested in electricity, and was constantly conducting chemical experiments, testing new dyes, trying to make synthetic diamonds and rubies, using the kitchen pots and pans, and, on one occasion at least, frightening his landlady out of her wits by causing a ferocious explosion. No one, it seems, ever ventured into his room without shouting up to inquire whether Mayhew was scientific or literary that day, for if he was scientific, the smell was sure to be poisonous.

Despite the variety of his talents and interests, the number of his friends, and the great amount of his published work, little is known of Henry Mayhew, little has ever been written about him. The *Dictionary of National Biography* provides scarcely more than a list of his publications. When he died the obituarists could find little to record. He is worthy of a better memorial.

Henry Mayhew was born on November 25, 1812. His father, Joshua Dorset Mayhew, was a wealthy solicitor, a partner in the successful firm of Mayhew, Johnson and Mayhew. He was also a strict, exacting man of regular habits and formidable manner. He had seven sons, and each in turn was taken into the family firm as an articled clerk; but only two of them remained to become partners. All the others abandoned the law for more congenial pursuits, and all of them, at one time or another, had reason to be thankful for the pound a week their father allowed them.

At the age of nine, in January, 1822, Henry Mayhew joined his two elder brothers at Westminster School, where he proved himself a boy of considerable talent but little application, doing no more work than he had to and receiving frequent floggings from the headmaster, Dr. Goodenough. After one particular flogging, decreed for his failure to finish

Telescope exhibitor

writing out five hundred lines of Virgil, he ran away from school. A few weeks later, shortly after his fifteenth birthday, he sailed to India as a midshipman aboard a tea clipper.

On his return from India—without money or even any trophies, apart from a tarantula preserved in rum—Henry decided that he had had enough of the sea and was ready to agree to his father's suggestion that he become an articled clerk in the family firm. But a lawyer's work did not appeal to him, and he spent as much time as he could out of the office, walking the streets of London. Indeed, he became so absorbed in this activity that one day he forgot to deliver an urgent document entrusted to his care, an oversight that almost resulted in his father's being committed for contempt of court and did result in his own dismissal not only from the firm but also from his home.

Having tried both the sea and the law without success, Mayhew, at the age of nineteen, took to journalism. With a former school friend, Gilbert à Beckett, he founded and edited a humorous paper, *Figaro in London,* a four-page weekly selling for a penny. The magazine, nearly all of which was written by the two editors themselves, was intended not merely to be funny but "pungently to portray the vices, improprieties and cant of the times by fair and honest attack." By contemporary standards it succeeded in both endeavors; it survived for eight years and achieved a reputation, despite its often coarse and usually feeble jokes, for responsible dramatic criticism and good-natured satire.

Long before the last issue of *Figaro in London* had appeared, Mayhew, from whose restless brain ideas shot forth like sparks from an anvil, had started another paper, a scissors-and-paste journal, *The Thief,* which was honest enough to admit what similar periodicals did not, that most of its contents had previously appeared elsewhere. *The Thief*'s first issue, published on April 21, 1832, promised that the paper would "always be amusing," but it never enjoyed the success of *Figaro in London.* It

Apple seller with her wares

lost so much money, in fact, that Mayhew was forced to flee from London to escape his creditors.

For a time he lived in a *hôtel meublé* in Paris on the pound a week his father allowed him. On his return, so he later said, he went to live as a hermit in Wales, studying, reading, spending half his allowance on board and lodging and the other half on his scientific works.

Although he seemed preoccupied with trying—and repeatedly failing—to make his fortune by some startling invention, he still managed to conceive a stream of ideas for literary projects. He wrote or collaborated on two burlettas, three knockabout farces, and numerous contributions to magazines. By the beginning of the 1840's, when he was permanently settled in London again, he had also developed the idea for a new periodical of his own for which he had chosen the title *Cupid,* had made a "dummy," and with characteristic enthusiasm and temerity had begun to assemble the staff, although he had not yet found a backer. He never found one; but *Cupid,* though stillborn, did serve as inspiration for a periodical that was to become one of the most famous and durable in the world.

So many journalists, printers, and engravers were present at the birth of *Punch* that a mass of conflicting claims subsequently arose as to who was responsible for its inception. But from the haze of tobacco smoke and the fumes of rum that surrounded these men in the rooms where they met, from the uncertain memories of numerous conversations and arguments, there emerges the indisputable fact that no one has a stronger claim to be considered the founder of *Punch* than Henry Mayhew.

It was he who interested its printer in the foundation of a magazine based partly on the projected *Cupid* and partly on the French satirical magazine *Charivari.* It was he who enlisted the help of Mark Lemon, a fellow contributor to *Bentley's Miscellany* and the convivial landlord of the Shakespeare's Head, a recognized meeting place of journalists and artists and their bohemian hangers-on. It was he who suggested its name over a bowl of punch at another tavern, the Edinburgh Castle. It was he who, along with Lemon and Stirling Coyne, a young Irish dramatic critic, was appointed one of its joint editors. And it was Mayhew who kept up the spirits of those involved in the venture during its early days when it seemed unlikely that the fledgling publication would survive.

Despite Mayhew's encouragement and good spirits, those who had more responsibility in financial matters were increasingly concerned by *Punch's* losses. Toward the end of 1842 it was decided that the magazine would have to be sold if a purchaser could be found, and a purchaser *was* found in the successful firm of Bradbury and Evans. Mayhew played little part in the negotiations. He was well known to be in no sense a businessman; and it was due mainly to the "eloquence" of Mark Lemon, so Frederick Evans said, that Bradbury and Evans were induced to take *Punch* over and pay its debts. They were also persuaded to reorganize its staff and to make Lemon the sole editor.

Mayhew felt himself grossly ill-treated. He had not only been responsible for starting the paper but had provided it with some of its best and most popular features. It was through his influence that Thackeray's reluctance to write for an "undignified vehicle of a shabby Fleet Street coterie" had at last been overcome. It had been mainly his idea to include an annual almanac, with a page for each month illustrated by lively, amusing drawings and filled with jokes —a suggestion that had led to a sudden and spectacular leap in sales. Anxious

not to lose the benefit of his lively mind, Bradbury and Evans asked Mayhew to stay on as "Suggestor-in-Chief." He agreed to do so, but his intimate friendship with Lemon was over.

For three more years Mayhew remained a contributor to *Punch,* but in 1846 he decided to break off all connection with the paper. It was not only his continuing antipathy for Lemon that finally led to his withdrawal; a more decisive reason was that Douglas Jerrold, now *Punch's* main contributor, was imposing upon it a bitter political bias that Mayhew found vindictive.

Leaving *Punch,* a paper that he looked upon with a jealously proprietorial regard, was a severe wrench for Mayhew, and his sense of injustice at being ousted by Lemon remained with him for the rest of his life. But as the numerous friends who were called upon to listen to his excited monologues had good cause to know, he had other irons in the fire. There were two projected series of educational books (only the first titles in each ever appeared); there were ideas for new magazines, new plays, new novels—projects that seemed for the moment inspirational but were likely to be dropped as suddenly as they were taken up. "He was brimming over with novel ideas," Henry Vizetelly recalled. "He would scheme and ponder all day long, but he abominated the labour of putting his ideas into tangible shape."

He would talk endlessly of books and people, of life and his scientific experiments, entertaining his friends late into the night. But however late it was when he went to bed, he always got up early to devise new schemes, develop new ideas, or make suggestions to fellow writers, dictating to his brothers Augustus or

Lucifer match girl

Horace or to his devoted wife, Jane.

He had married Jane in 1844, and according to Henry Vizetelly, she was "deeply attached to him." She was the eldest daughter of his former colleague Douglas Jerrold, and seems by every account to have been a charming woman, patient and forbearing—as, indeed, she had need to be. Mayhew not only used her as a secretary but left her to confront his creditors; and since most of his letters came from such people, he handed them all over to her.

He had occasional successes: for instance, the humorous novel *The Greatest Plague of Life,* which he wrote in collaboration with Augustus. But for all the critical success of the book, in which there is a social awareness lacking in most Victorian novels of its sort, and for all his inventiveness and bursts of energy, Mayhew's financial fortunes did not prosper. In February, 1847, with debts of more than 2,000 pounds, he found himself involved in bankruptcy proceedings. His income for 1844 and 1845 was declared to be no more than 300 pounds each year; in 1846 increased earnings of 625 pounds had prompted him to take a larger house, the Shrubbery at Parson's Green, and to contract "large debts for furnishing and ornamenting the premises in a way that was not warrented by his position." He disingenuously excused himself by pleading that he had expected Bradbury and Evans to compensate him for his retirement from *Punch,* a magazine created by himself; and he went on to contend that he would never have been forced into bankruptcy had not Mark Lemon failed to honor an agreement to pay him for his help with various farces they had written together and from

Doctor Bokany, herbalist

Street acrobats

which Lemon had taken all the profits.

Narrowly escaping a prison sentence, Mayhew returned to writing with a new vigor and determination. Within the next few years he turned out an astonishing amount of work: fairy tales, biographies for children, more humorous novels, a study of the Mormons. But as soon as the money came in it was spent, and Mayhew's friends and relations were continually called upon to get him out of some new scrape. "I must be in London on Saturday and sometimes on Monday," runs one characteristic letter from his father-in-law to Dickens's friend and biographer, John Forster, "in re Mayhew, whom God make wiser."

In 1858 his father died; but, having recognized his son's improvidence, he was careful not to let him get his hands on any capital, making provisions instead for his daughter-in-law to receive a small income in trust for him. So Mayhew went on working as hard, and erratically, as ever. In the 1860's he was in Germany, having decided to write a book about the boyhood of Martin Luther, which appeared in 1865. Previous visits to Germany had resulted in two travel books, and this longer sojourn inspired the more successful and highly entertaining *German Life and Manners as seen in Saxony at the Present Day* (1884), a two-volume work dedicated to the author's "dear wife," "literally my *right* hand," as her husband called her, "scribbling to my dictation, often night and day."

Jane Mayhew seems to have remained devoted to her husband. Some years before, she had borne him a son, Athol,

and a daughter, Amy, and Mayhew appears to have been as fond a father as he was a husband. In 1870 he and Athol were in Metz together reporting on the Franco-Prussian War.

Yet, successful and resourceful though he proved to be as a war correspondent, Henry Mayhew had no further good fortune as a writer when the war was over. He published a mediocre book on the young Benjamin Franklin in 1870; in the same year he promoted yet another periodical, which did not long survive, and contributed to a collection entitled *London Characters* that had but a limited success; he even tried to obtain employment as a ghost writer for a well-known horse trainer. In 1871 he prepared a report on workingmen's clubs; and in 1874 he and Athol wrote a comedy, *Mont Blanc,* which was a disastrous failure. In 1880 his wife died, and thereafter he wrote little. He himself died, in Charlotte Street, Bloomsbury, on July 25, 1887.

There were a few short obituaries, inaccurate and misleading. The *Illustrated London News* reported that if the author of *London Labour and the London Poor* had died twenty years earlier, his passing would have aroused widespread notice and sympathy; as it was, the world at large seemed to have forgotten him. So, too, have Mayhew's plays and novels been forgotten, as have his travel books and children's books, his fairy tales and biographies, his magazines and almanacs. But that unique survey, *London Labour and the London Poor,* has assured his fame as one of the great Victorians.

The survey was first undertaken as a journalistic enterprise, and never, even in its later stages, did Mayhew have any official support. At one time, it seemed that the project, like most of Mayhew's ventures, would never be completed. The *Morning Chronicle* ceased publication of the articles following a complaint from one of their advertisers, a Regent Street tailor, that he had been libeled by Mayhew in a paragraph that exposed the dreadful conditions of his shop. Thereupon, Mayhew himself issued the

articles as a periodical selling at twopence for each weekly installment. In 1851 the first two volumes of the collected articles were published as *London Labour and the London Poor,* but the promised remainder of the work did not appear immediately, for Mayhew had become involved in a dispute with a printer who succeeded in interrupting further publication by litigation in chancery. In 1856 the work was continued, as a supposedly "new periodical on London and Londoners," under the title *The Great World of London;* but before he had finished the last part of the work—"The Criminal Prisons of London"—Mayhew went abroad, perhaps to escape his creditors again. The publishers of the final volume, which appeared in 1862, were forced to explain that owing to Mr. Mayhew's absence from England they had been obliged to arrange for the final 150-odd pages to be written by Mr. John Binny. So at last, thirteen years after its inception, the great work was finished.

It begins with an account of the London street sellers, the most numerous of whom were the costermongers, who dealt in fish, fruit, and vegetables. Mayhew estimated that there were no less than thirty thousand of these men—in a total population in 1851 of three and a quarter million—and that the number was growing each year. Each day the costermongers attended one or another of the markets to buy their goods, which they then sold from either a stationary stall or a barrow, cart, or tray.

They were rough, quarrelsome, illiterate, a vital set of men much given to fighting, drinking, and gambling, to tattooing their arms and throwing bricks at

Punch and Judy showmen

policemen. Anxious to keep the secrets of their trade from the police and potential rivals, they spoke to each other in an esoteric language, incomprehensible to the uninitiated, that involved the use of a cryptic vocabulary and an ability to pronounce words backward. Few of them could read or write; few troubled to marry the women they lived with; most—though not above cheating their customers—were honest among themselves and kind to their children and donkeys.

They were fond of dancing at "twopenny-hops," jigging and jumping and leaping at clog-hornpipes and polkas, flash jigs and pipe dances. They were regular visitors at the theatres and penny concerts, the dog fights, above all at the taprooms; and everywhere they went they gambled. They bet on skittles and fights, on shove-halfpenny and three-up, on pigeon races and on card games such as all fives, cribbage, and put. They sat for hours, full of beer and shrouded in tobacco, thumbing their torn and filthy cards from which the symbols had almost been effaced, muttering to each other in that curious language of theirs, breaking off now and again to watch a boxing match (all self-respecting landlords provided gloves), to have another drink, or to listen to one of their more literate companions recount the latest episode in Reynold's "Mysteries of the Court."

Their children began working with them at an early age, usually before they were seven, watching the cart and the donkey, mastering the tricks of the trade —how to swell oranges, boil prunes, bake filberts—and learning to shout their wares: "Ni-ew mackerel, six a shilling! . . . All large and alive-O, new sprats, penny a plate! . . . Penny a bunch turnips!"

When they were about thirteen the boys started in business on their own with a woman of their own, settling the arrangement by giving the girl a silk neckerchief. The London costermongers were inordinately proud of

Ethiopian serenaders

their silk neckerchiefs—King's-men they called them—and, indeed, of all their clothes. The men wore long cord waistcoats with huge and numerous pockets and shining brass buttons, trousers fitting tightly at the knee and billowing out over highly polished boots, and a worsted skullcap or a cloth cap pulled down low on one side.

Costermongers were but one of the innumerable hawkers who made a living, or at least some sort of subsistence, in the London streets. There were sellers of cooked food and sellers of drink, piemen and muffinmen, spice and rhubarb girls and hot-eel boys, mice exhibitors and snake swallowers, penny-gaff clowns and stilt-vaulters, crossing sweepers and scavengers, street mechanics and flagstone artists, reciters and penny-profile cutters, rag and bottle men, dog finders, packmen and cheap johns, running patterers and chanters, old men with trays of cough drops and hot elder wine, old women with pickled whelks and cress, boys with oranges and nuts, girls with boiled puddings. There were Irish cat-meat dealers, Italian organ boys, Jewish clothesmen, French singing women, Dutch buy-a-broom girls, Highland bagpipe players, and Ethiopian serenaders.

Thousands lived by what they could pick up on the streets, along the waterfront, and in the sewers. In the early morning they could be seen moving about with bags on their shoulders looking for bits of wood and coal, cigar ends, rags, bones, and dog dung, which was known as "pure" because the Bermondsey tanners used it for purifying leather.

The bone pickers and rag gatherers went out armed with a spiked stick that they poked into piles of dust and rubbish in back streets, picking up anything they could sell and placing it in their greasy bags, making their breakfast on bits of bread they came across or on the meat they found sticking to the bones they gathered. They covered about twenty-five miles each day in the course of their searches, taking eight or nine hours to do so, and selling what they had for about sixpence a day.

The pure-finders were rather better paid than most of the scavengers, since a bucketful could be sold for as much as a shilling and twopence, and many of the more active collectors could be sure of taking home between five and six shillings a week. This, however, was a poor wage compared with the sums earned by those who scavenged in the sewers. These men, London's "toshers," thought themselves unfortunate if they did not make two pounds a week. Toshers, in fact, were almost an elite among scavengers. They entered the sewers on the river's shore and came out on occasions laden with copper and silver coins, bits of iron, ropes and bones, even plated spoons and ladles, silver-handled knives, and jewelry.

They were not begrudged their fortune, though, for the work was extremely dangerous. Most of the sewers were incalculably old and ramshackle and the brickwork constantly threatened to collapse. There was also the risk

"Long-song" seller

of drowning, for the tide often rushed in without warning at the speed of a mountain torrent; and there was the ever-present possibility of being suffocated or poisoned by the foul vapors in the branch sewers where a man had to crouch to move along. Since no one knew the sewers' extent, there were many tales of toshers having lost their way and dying of exhaustion and hunger; and, since the sewers swarmed with rats, there were even more terrible stories of the scavengers being over-powered by them and of their skeletons being discovered a few days later picked clean of skin and flesh.

Yet, despite the dangers of their life and the supposedly poisonous qualities of the air in which they worked, toshers were a cheerful and healthy group, car-rying on their work until they were sev-enty or eighty years old, well fed and well satisfied with their lot.

Far less fortunate were the "mud larks," who scavenged on the riverfront at low tide. Most mud larks were very old or very young or badly crippled, as none but the weak would undertake such hard and filthy work for so poor a return. Even the bone pickers earned twice as much as they did: a mud lark considered himself lucky if he could sell all he had found in a day for a half-penny.

They went down into the mud by the banks of the Thames carrying old hats or rusty kettles, poking about for pieces of coal or copper nails, their clothes a collection of old rags as stiff as boards, their feet bare and in danger of being cut on fragments of buried glass. In winter,

Sewer scavenger

Jack Black, royal ratcatcher

the greatest pleasure they knew was to stand in the hot water that ran down from the factories and warm their feet.

The little watercress girls lived a life scarcely less terrible. At the age of seven or eight they would get up before dawn to go down to Farringdon Market to haggle with the saleswomen. In the cold weather they shivered in their cotton dresses and threadbare shawls as they tied up the bunches, and their fingers ached as they washed the leaves at the pump. They walked the streets crying, "Water-Cresses, four bunches a penny, Water-Cresses!" and on an average day they would make three or four pence. One of them, aged eight, said:

I used to go to school, too; but I wasn't there long. I've forgot all about it now, it's such a time ago; and mother took me away because the master whacked me . . . he hit me three times, ever so hard, across the face with his cane. . . . The creases is so bad now. . . . They're so cold, people won't buy 'em; for when I goes up to them, they say, "They'll freeze our bellies." . . . We never goes home to breakfast till we've sold out; but, if it's very late, then I buys a penn'orth of pudden, which is very nice with gravy. I don't know hardly one of the people, as goes to Farring-don, to talk to; they never speaks to me, so I don't speak to them. We children never play down there, 'cos we're thinking of our living. No; people never pities me in the street—ex-cepting one gentleman, and he says, says he, "What do you do out so soon in the morn-ing?" but he gave me nothink—he only walked away. . . . No; I never see any children crying, it's no use. . . .

I always give mother my money, she's so very good to me. She don't often beat me. . . . She's very poor and goes out cleaning rooms sometimes. . . . I ain't got no father, he's a

father-in-law. No; mother ain't married again—he's a father-in-law. He grinds scis-sors, and he's very good to me. No; I don't mean by that that he says kind things to me, for he never hardly speaks. When I gets home, after selling creases . . . I puts the room to rights. . . . I cleans the chairs, though there's only two to clean. I takes a tub and scrubbing-brush and flannel, and scrubs the floor. . . .

I don't have no dinner. Mother gives me two slices of bread-and-butter and a cup of tea for breakfast, and then I go to tea, and has the same. We has meat of a Sunday, and, of course, I should like to have it every day. . .

All the money I earns I puts in a club and draws it out to buy clothes with. It's better than spending it in sweet-stuff, for them as has a living to earn. Besides it's like a child to care for sugar-sticks, and not like one who's got a living and vittals to earn. . . . I'm past eight, I am. I don't know nothing about what I earns during the year, I only knows how many pennies goes to a shilling, and two ha'pence goes to a penny, and four fardens goes to a penny. I knows, too, how many far-dens goes to tuppence—eight. That's as much as I wants to know for the markets.

Compared with some London chil-dren, this one was content. At least she had a home and had found work to do. Hundreds of other children had neither. One was a boy of thirteen whose clothes were so scant and torn that most of his chest was bare, and what he had wrapped around himself for trousers covered only one of his legs. On one foot he wore an old shoe tied around his in-step with a piece of ribbon, on the other a woman's discarded boot. His face was swollen with the cold. His father had died when he was three years old; his mother, who had gone out begging, was dead, too. He had sixpence in his pocket when she died, but he couldn't help cry-ing to think he'd lost his mother, and he cried about it still. He'd gone out beg-ging on his own:

I begged, but sometimes wouldn't get a far-thing in a day; often walking about the streets all night. I am very weak—starving to death. I never stole anything. A boy wanted me to go with him to pick a gentleman's pocket, but I wouldn't. The boy asked me to do it to get into prison. He was starving about the streets like me. I never slept in a bed since I've been in London. I generally slept under the dry arches in West Street, where they're building houses—I mean the arches for the cellars. I begged chiefly from the Jews about Petticoat Lane for they all give away bread that their children leave—pieces of crust and such-like.

Children who could rely on help or encouragement from adults usually found some sort of work that would pay for more than crusts of bread—even if it was only selling nuts and oranges at the doors of theatres at night, sweeping crossings, hanging around cab stands in the hope of payment for holding a horse or opening a door. Sometimes they hawked fusees—"Buy a fuzee to light your cigar, your honour, sir. A row of lights for a halfpence." But the competition in such pursuits was intense, and for those endeavors in which a better living might be had, some skill or capital was necessary.

There was a ready market for goldfish in the streets, but the fish had to be bought from a dealer in Kingsland Road or Billingsgate; bird nests, snakes, and frogs also sold well, but experience was required to find them. One young man sold twenty bird nests a week at two or three pence apiece, and snakes for five shillings a pound—either for their skins or to a gentleman in Theobald's Road who dissected them. He sold good frogs, too, for a shilling a dozen to the French hotel in Leicester Square and in the streets as well—"many people swallows young frogs, they're reckoned very good things to clear the inside"—but collecting his wares was hard and skilled work, and he had few rivals.

There was good money in dredging the river for corpses, but you had to have pots and pans; you could become a

Vagrant mother and children

hurdy-gurdy woman, but you had to have the instrument to churn out its fearful noise. You could make a reasonable living tumbling in Waterloo Place after the opera, or in the Haymarket where the street girls were—though they didn't part with money themselves, they told their gentlemen to—but you had to be able to do it well and not everyone could learn. You might decide to become a rat catcher, since there was an enormous demand for rats by "sporting gentlemen" who attended such establishments as the King's Head, Compton Street, Soho, to watch them being killed by dogs. But long experience was required to catch a rat without getting yourself bitten to the bone. Many men made a good income out of dealing in coal, for there were thousands who could afford no more than a few lumps at a time, and a ton or so bought from a merchant and stored in a back room would soon bring in a handsome profit. But first you had to have the money for the merchant.

Although the poorer families used little coal, more than three and a half million tons of it were burned in London every year. This provided regular work both for the chimney sweeps, who could make as much as a pound a week in winter, and for the dustmen, who were paid eight pence a load by dust contractors and could usually manage to cart away to the dust yards at least two, and perhaps three, loads a day.

The dustmen walked down the street in their hooded caps, leading a horse and box cart and crying "Dust oy-eh! Dust oy-eh!," stopping outside houses where there was dust to collect, filling their buckets from the dust bins, and emptying the loads into the cart. The refuse was trundled away to the dust yard where, amid pigs rooting about for bits of offal and hens picking at cabbage leaves, men, women, and children would be hard at work on the mountainous heaps of rubbish with iron sieves to separate the "brieze" from the "soil": the "brieze," or coarse cindery dust, was dispatched to the brickfields, the finer "soil" sold as manure. Broken bricks,

Mud lark

old boots, kettles, rags, bones, and oyster shells—all found their appropriate market, to the great profit of the dust contractors.

The laborers on the heaps stood in dust up to their waists, the women in black bonnets, their dirty cotton dresses tucked up behind them, banging their sieves against leather aprons. At the larger dust yards—one of the biggest was on the banks of the Regent's Canal —there were usually well over a hundred people hard at work.

Although little or no skill was required to work for a dust contractor, a dustman frequently earned more in a week than many a skilled worker could. A chairmaker, for example, would work from six o'clock in the morning until nine or ten at night, stopping ten minutes for breakfast at eight o'clock, twenty minutes for dinner, and eight minutes for tea, eating in the room where he worked. He worked the same hours every Saturday and for forty Sundays during the year. Including the time spent carting his finished articles to the purchaser, a chairmaker might well work a hundred hours a week, year in, year out.

The thousands of men who worked in the London docks were no more fortunate. The dock area, a sprawling muddle of warehouses, wharfs, courts, alleys, lodging houses, marine-supply stores, public houses, shoe markets, sailmakers' yards, quays, factories, ropeworks, brothels, chapels, sheds, and workshops, covered an area of more than ninety acres. In this turmoil, and surrounded by a ferment of smells—hides, rum, dry rot, burning oil, stale beer, wine, sulfur, tobacco, fish, and rotting rope—three thousand casual laborers of all sorts and nationalities struggled daily to find work. When the gates opened in the morning, they streamed toward the foremen, shouting, jumping scuffling, waving their arms in a frantic attempt to gain their notice and a hard day's work for a half-a-crown pay. There was never enough work for all of them; some came every day for weeks on end and were never called, relying upon the others for enough food to keep them alive until their turn came. Most of them supplied power for the huge wheels that operated the cranes, six to eight of them inside each wheel walking up the battens like convicts on a treadmill. Others unloaded cargo or carried bales of goods across the quays.

Not content with minutely describing the working conditions of the London poor, Mayhew also took his readers into the crowded warrens where they found shelter at night. An omnibus driver or conductor, earning a more regular wage than most, might live in relative comfort in Battersea or Clapham in a couple of rooms with clean floors and windows, picture postcards and prints of Jack Sheppard and Dick Turpin stuck on the walls, a few pieces of crockery, a tin tray and a piece of looking glass on the mantelpiece, a cloth on the table and a sheet on the bed. But most of the London poor lived in conditions far worse than this. Many of them were crowded into rooms with ceilings the color of old leather, with broken windows stuffed with paper and broken furniture beyond repair, rotting floorboards covered perhaps by three or four old mats tied together to form a carpet, sleeping five in a bed or on a flock mattress (crawling with bugs) on the floor.

Tens of thousands slept in cheap lodging houses down by the docks. The charge was twopence a night for a bundle of rags on a bunk and the use of a kitchen where there was a fire on which residents could cook their meals. For a penny reduction in the fee, one could sleep on the floor of the kitchen, and many did so, women as well as men, girls as well as boys, most of

them having taken the precaution of getting drunk if they could afford it, for otherwise there was no sleep to be had.

Mayhew's survey, although it relentlessly conveys the continuing tragedy of the London poor, also shows us how so many of them contrived to enjoy life, how marvelously they responded to what small pleasures they could afford. He describes them sitting down with relish to a meal of pea soup and pickled whelks, of hot eels, sheep's-trotters, and boiled meat pudding with plenty of pepper. He shows them crowding around the baked-potato sellers who stood at every street corner with the muffinmen and the men with ginger beer fountains, chestnut stoves, or trays of sugar-sticks.

Cab driver with his whip

He conducts us through the open street markets of Whitecross Street and the New Cut, Lambeth, where treacle rock and yellow haddocks, russet apples and Yarmouth bloaters, purple pickled cabbage and oysters, were lit up by oil lamps or candles stuck inside turnips or sieves. He introduces us to the numerous street entertainers: the conjurers in Jermyn Street, the fire-eaters in Gray's Inn Lane, the Punch and Judy men in Leicester Square and Tottenham Court Road, the fantoccini men who manipulated dancing dolls and comic skeletons, and the exhibitors of peep shows, mechanical figures, and telescopes (a penny a peep). And he takes us into a tavern to see a rat match in which five hundred rats were slaughtered.

Even more popular than the rat

matches was the theatre. Many men whose income was less than two pounds a week spent three or four evenings a week at the theatre, taking their wives with them and cheering or condemning the performance with all the lusty partiality of Shakespeare's day.

Throughout the performance the spectators munched on pig's-trotters and ham sandwiches that were sold in the intervals, cracked nuts, sucked oranges, drank porter, greeted complaints that people behind could not see with threats to throw them over the railings, wiped the sweat from their faces with crumpled playbills, shouted at the actors to speak up, encouraged them with cries of "Bray-vo, Vincent. Go it, my tulip!" and insisted, each time a favorite tune was played, on singing the words to it or clapping out its rhythm.

And for those who could not afford the theatre, there were "penny gaffs," upper floors of shops that had been turned into places of entertainment, where disreputable performers danced and sang to the accompaniment of a noisy band. The audience at these performances consisted mostly of women and young girls and boys: the boys lighting their pipes at the gas jets that spluttered on each side of the makeshift proscenium or tickling the girls in the seats in front of them; the girls, some of them only eight years of age, laughing and shouting, clapping their hands, waving the shabby feathers in their bonnets backward and forward rhythmically.

Some of these girls, even at so early an age, were professional prostitutes. Mayhew estimated that about half of London's eighty thousand prostitutes were under fifteen, and that there were thousands of other girls in their early teens who were part-time prostitutes known as "dolly mops," and who were kept, by those who could afford the luxury, in apartments in such respectable enclaves as St. John's Wood, Brompton, and Regent's Park.

More than half the professional prostitutes, so Mayhew tells us, worked in brothels. There were, he calculated, nearly three thousand of these, the most squalid of which were down by the docks, where, in certain courts off Bluegate Fields, every room in every house was given over to prostitution, where the smell of opium lay sweet and heavy in the air, where the only items of furniture were damp paillasses and broken bedsteads, and where some of the women earned no more than their predecessors had in Boswell's day.

The prostitutes who worked in the parks, however, although they were the cheapest to be found outside the East End, considered themselves unfortunate if they did not earn two or three pounds a week, and many earned five or six. The French girls, most of whom lived in lodgings in Queen Street off Regent Street and charged their customers a guinea each, made on the average twice as much. But even this was a paltry sum when compared with the income of the girls who wandered outside the clubs in Pall Mall or frequented the more fashionable night houses that were located in the Haymarket area.

Mayhew's description of the London prostitutes, and of the bawds, pimps, panders, and bullies who lived on their earnings, are contained in the first part of the fourth volume of his book, which is otherwise devoted entirely to those tens of thousands of Londoners who lived wholly or partly by crime or begging.

Here, as elsewhere, Mayhew exposes but he does not preach; he reveals but he never condemns. And this is his great strength as a social inquirer. He shares with Dickens (strangely, there is no record of the two ever meeting) a regard for the existing moral code and a belief that those who transgressed it must surely end in misery. But he was far ahead of his time in insisting that any steps toward social reform must be firmly based on detailed, dispassionate investigation of a sort that had never been done before but would be commonplace later. He was, in fact, one of the great pioneers of social science and criminal ecology. His volumes are the prototype of later surveys, but they are written with such understanding, such fascina-

tion, so refreshing a lack of either condescension or humbug, such vivid immediacy that they are unique: the very colors and smells of the East End come rising out of their pages.

The wonderfully evocative effect that Mayhew succeeds in creating is due, not so much to his skill as a journalist, novelist, and playwright, as to the warmth and attractiveness of his coaxing personality, his ability to get his subjects to talk frankly and naturally. The engraver Ebenezer Landells recorded that he once saw Mayhew at work talking to a costermonger, drawing his story out of him, leaving Augustus and his brother-in-law, William Jerrold, to put in a word or comment so that it seemed more like a conversation

Costermonger

than an interview, and meanwhile relying on another brother, Horace, to take down everything that was said.

In the correspondence that the early installments of his survey evoked, Mayhew made his own position clear: he was not connected with any social or political party; he was merely "a collector of facts." But what he did want to show was "the importance of the poor and the working-class as members of society"; he wanted the workingman to "get his just share of the produce" of his labor, and he wanted to see trade unionism prosper. As the work progressed, specific targets came under attack: common lodging houses and the sweat system; thoughtless and indiscriminate almsgiving; the fearful complacency of the upper and middle classes, who knew

little or nothing about the effects of the Irish immigration that had followed the famine of 1846, or of the cholera epidemic of 1848-49, who had no conception of the effects of the decline of the railway boom that had swamped the labor market with out-of-work navvies, and little idea of the aspirations of the Chartists and the calls for revolution, or of criminality as a way of life.

It cannot be claimed for *London Labour and the London Poor* that its publication led to immediate specific reforms. Many of his readers, in their selfishness or complacency, comforted themselves with the belief that, shocking though poverty was in London, poverty in most large cities in Britain was quite as bad, and that in the industrial north it was even worse. They consoled themselves with the knowledge that Mayhew's writings revealed not merely the degradation of poverty but the heartening resilience and dogged resolution of the English character, the capacity of the impoverished Cockney to survive in squalor and even to regard his position in society with a humorous, wry detachment. Some of them, like John Podsnap in *Our Mutual Friend,* preferred not to notice that alarming mass of people swirling densely and dangerously at their feet: "I don't want to know about it; I don't choose to discuss it; I don't admit it."

But there were others, gradually growing in number, to whom Mayhew's work was an inspiration, who recognized that the lives of the poor could no longer be disregarded. And in later Victorian times, as slums were cleared away and institutions founded, as new housing projects got under way, reformers like Lord Shaftesbury, Sir Edwin Chadwick, and Octavia Hill lived to see the beginning of new hope for those whom Mayhew had so vividly and piteously depicted walking the "cold, wet, shelterless midnight streets" of London.

Among the plenitude of topics that interest Christopher Hibbert are kings, highwaymen, Italians from the Medici to Mussolini, and nineteenth-century London.

Dead to the World

Look closely at this corpse. It's trying to tell you something

"The corpse that you see here is that of M. Bayard, inventor of the process of which you have just seen, or are about to see, the wonderful results. To my knowledge, this ingenious and indefatigable researcher has worked for nearly three years to perfect his invention.

"The Academy, the King, and all those who have seen his pictures have admired them just as you admire them right now, even though he himself still considers them imperfect. Much honor has come his way, but not one sou. The government which has already given too much to M. Daguerre, declared itself unable to do a thing for M. Bayard, and the unfortunate creature has drowned himself. Oh human fickleness! For a long time artists, scientists, and the press took an interest in him, but now he has been lying in the Morgue for days, and no one has recognized or claimed him. Ladies and gentlemen, let's talk of something else so that your sense of smell is not upset, for as you have probably noticed, the face and hands have already started to decompose."

The man who took the photograph opposite, the man who wrote the inscription printed below it, and the "corpse" itself were one and the same: Hippolyte Bayard, the as yet unrecognized inventor of photography in France. At the time that Bayard posed as a drowned man, in October, 1840, he was thirty-nine years old, a minor bureaucrat in the Ministry of Finance, and a man who, in his spare time, had devised a method for making permanent photographic images on paper. The reason his work is so little known can be traced directly to his character, for Hippolyte Bayard was a timid soul, and his timidity assured the neglect of which he complained.

If the average Frenchman had been asked in 1840 about pictures made in the camera, he would have said without hesitation that they were the invention of Louis Daguerre. For on August 19, 1839, with the announcement of Daguerre's method of exposing silvered plates to light and developing a latent image by means of mercury vapor, all Paris was seized by daguerreotypomania. One observer reported that an hour after the details of Daguerre's experiments had been made public "all the opticians' shops were besieged, but could not rake together enough instruments to satisfy the onrushing army of would-be daguerreotypists; a few days later you could see in all the squares of Paris three-legged dark-boxes planted in front of churches and palaces."

Popular as it was, daguerreotypy was only one among many methods then being developed for making fixed images in the camera. Once Daguerre's method was publicized, inventors of photographic processes popped up everywhere. The English inventor William Henry Fox Talbot claimed priority for his method since he had succeeded in making the first paper negative in 1835. Our "corpse" only wished to be recognized as an independent inventor of photography and it is a matter of record that Bayard had, in fact, made photographs—negatives and positives on paper—months before Talbot and Daguerre revealed their techniques.

We know little of Bayard's life apart from the records of his experiments and the photographs themselves—some six hundred of them—that are preserved in the collection of the Société Française de Photographie. Born the son of a justice of the peace on January 20, 1801, Bayard grew up in the small town of Breteuil-sur-Noye, north of Paris. He worked for a time in a local notary's office and was good friends with a fellow clerk, Edmond Geoffroy, who wanted to become an actor. The two young men set off for Paris—Geoffroy to success as a member of the Comédie Française, Bayard to take a clerk's job in the Ministry of Finance. Bayard liked

to draw, Geoffroy was a painter, and the two soon became acquainted with several artists and engravers.

Perhaps it was from his artist friends that Bayard first heard of Daguerre's photographic experiments. In any case, we know that he began to work at photography in earnest in January, 1839, when it became known that Daguerre had succeeded in developing, by chemical means, the image produced on a metal plate in the camera. Bayard was determined to achieve similar results with paper. By February 5, he had made some imperfect negative images on paper; by March 20, he had produced his first direct positive on paper in the camera. (Curiously, no one in the early days of photography was interested in negative images, from which an unlimited number of positive images

In 1855 Bayard took another picture of himself, this time fully clothed.

could be printed. This negative-positive process—the basis of photography today—seemed a roundabout way to achieve the desired result.)

On May 20, 1839, Bayard formally presented the results of his work to Dominique François Arago, a noted physicist and astronomer who was an influential member of the Chamber of Deputies. Then, at a charity bazaar on June 24, Bayard exhibited thirty paper positives, most of them still lifes. In just six months Hippolyte Bayard, working only in his spare time and with a poor lens, had achieved two important photographic firsts: he had made direct positives on paper and he had held the world's first photographic exhibit.

In 1840 Bayard finally revealed the secret of his method: "Ordinary letter paper having been prepared [with silver chloride] and blackened by light, I soak it for several sec-

onds in a solution of potassium iodide; then putting the paper on a piece of slate, I place it in the camera. After the image is formed, I wash this paper in a solution of hyposulfite of soda and again in pure hot water and dry it in the dark."

Bayard's lack of confidence was indicated by the fact that he dried his prints in the dark, even though they had been fixed by "hypo." His caution was unnecessary: after more than a hundred years his photographs are in perfect condition. Moreover, they exhibit an aesthetic sense, a delicate luminosity, and a range of tone unusual in such early work. Even in his corpse photograph, he has carefully draped his naked torso and hung an enormous sun hat on the wall to balance the composition. Whether he photographed boats on the Seine, the windmills of Montmartre, the streets of Paris, flower pots in his garden, or himself, Bayard looked through the lens with the eye of an artist.

The corpse must surely be the world's first photographic joke. Bayard's body, glistening and white except for his suntanned face and hands, seems truly dead. We know, of course, that no morgue would be equipped with flowered drapery or a sun hat, still . . . Certainly it was a good way of pointing out Bayard's resentment of Daguerre and the French government.

That resentment was justified. Daguerre, in his eagerness to make a commercial success of the daguerreotype, enlisted the support of the scientist Arago, who finally, in July, 1839, persuaded the Chamber of Deputies to buy Daguerre's invention and give him a large pension. When Bayard appeared in his office in May, Arago must have been surprised and somewhat annoyed to discover that Daguerre's method was not the only successful photographic method around. Even so, since he was in the midst of advising the French government to buy one invention, it would hardly do to promote a similar invention. To discourage Bayard from publishing his method, Arago recommended that he be given six hundred francs to buy a better lens, an offer that the self-effacing Bayard meekly accepted.

Daguerre retired to the country with his earnings, leaving others to perfect his process. Bayard continued to take photographs when he was not at his job with the Finance Ministry and gained a modest reputation for his work among a small group of artists and friends. In 1842 the Société d'Encouragement pour l'Industrie Nationale bestowed a prize of three thousand francs on him, and in 1863 he was made a chevalier of the Légion d'Honneur. The corpse had quickened, and one day it would have the recognition it deserved.   —PRISCILLA FLOOD

If you think you hear superclones
in the rising drumbeat of genetic engineering, listen again
—and reconsider the story of

Man and His Best Friend

By ANTHONY SMITH

FIRST MURDERER: We are men, my liege.

MACBETH: Ay, in the catalogue ye go for men;

As hounds and greyhounds, mongrels,
    spaniels, curs,

Shoughs, water-rugs, and demi-wolves,
    are clept

All by the name of dogs. . . .

        MACBETH, ACT III, SCENE 1

It is possible, even within the arrogance of the twentieth century, to be amazed at the capabilities of earlier generations of men. By and large we are ignorant of the workings of modern things, of television tubes, transistors, and nuclear reactors; but, if the truth be admitted, previous and more fundamental discoveries made by simpler men are just as mysterious to us. How many of us, confronted by eager tribesmen wishing to leap ahead of their Stone Age toil, could make cement for them, or any metal or alloy, or glass, or even a brick that did not crumble into dust before our eyes? Yet we reserve for our early ancestors bemused condescension. We smile at their Neolithic simplicity, yet we could not make a flint arrowhead with one-hundredth of the grace they achieved. We smirk at those primitives who lived in caves, and yet, by some strange magic, these same primitives not only painted exquisitely but used dyes that are aglow to this day.

Such conceit on our part makes it hard for us to realize how much was achieved in the centuries before Christ was born. It is arguable, in fact, that there were more crucial innovations before that date than after. For example, the frontispiece of *The Neolithic Revolution* by Sonia Cole is a conjectural drawing of Jericho. It is harvest time. The men are cutting the einkorn, a kind of wheat. There are domesticated goats nearby, and the field is irrigated by spring water flowing along a ditch. The time of all this activity is nine thousand years ago. There is not, but there could well have been, a domestic dog watching the scene. Moreover, it need not have been some vague mongrel, but a creature of a breed and distinction fit for any hearthrug of today.

It should come as a jolt to our belief in the recentness of things that all the main groups of dogs were created long before Christ had appeared; in fact, they already existed when written history was making its first appearance. The breeding of dogs is ancient, and modern breeders have added little to the work done by the end of the Neolithic period.

There are several points of interest in the story of dog evolution. First, although these animals are still happily able to identify one of their kind, there has been tremendous adaptive radiation (that is, evolution of characteristics in response to various environments). There is curly hair, straight hair, wiry hair, silky hair; there are long faces, compressed faces, floppy ears, erect ears. There is a world of difference in the tail alone. As for weight, the Chihuahua can be confronted by a mastiff forty times its size. Second, most of this differentiation has been deliberately caused by man for his own purposes. Man has curtailed the random mating of dogs and has demonstrated the extraordinary variability inherent in the species (for it is just one species).

The dog story is also, to some degree, an accelerated version of mankind's own history. When men were banding together to form large village communities, they brought their dogs with them. Since then, both have experienced, in similar fashion, cultural and environmental changes—canned food, heated rooms, soft furnishings, urban compression, disease control. But dogs, with their quicker breeding cycle, have passed through some four thousand generations while man has experienced a tenth of that number. It is these facts, according to John Paul Scott and John L. Fuller, who have studied the relationship between genetics and the behavior of dogs, that suggest a hypothesis: "The genetic consequences of civilized living have been intensified in

Wolf on the prowl

From Savage to Snoopy

In form and function, in fact and fantasy, the dog has come a long way. Neolithic canines were hunters; the Egyptian jackal was a god. Pompeiians warned, "Beware of the Dog"; medieval men taught it to perform. As pampered pets, dogs inspired Reynolds and comforted Freud. Now they are lovable caricatures, thanks to Disney, Thurber, Lassie, and, good grief, Charles Schulz.

Neolithic hunting dog

Anubis, Egyptian god

the dog, and therefore the dog should give us some idea of the genetic future of mankind."

There is another important point. Evolution, or rapid genetic change, happens fastest when a population is divided into small isolated groups that have occasional genetic contact with each other. This was precisely the condition of mankind ten thousand years ago when dogs were becoming a part of each isolated scene. Trading, war, or friendly association between each group permitted a degree of genetic involvement between the dogs of one community and the dogs next door. Tribes of American Indians, for instance, with living areas spaced far apart, each had their own breeds of dog. These breeds were not greatly different from those of neighboring tribes, but across the continent the differences were intense. So, too, in earlier times with the fairly isolated, semi-independent groups of people that were the ancestors of us all.

Then came the Neolithic revolution, that tremendous upsurge when mankind took off in its present direction. It was an extraordinary age. Neolithic man, who should be given more credit than he normally is, subjected wild creatures and plants to his selection. As Sonia Cole puts it, "Every food plant of major importance to mankind was grown in the Neolithic stage of culture, just as all the main animals reared for meat today were domesticated during that period."

Various breeds of dog were dotted everywhere. They had been nurtured in isolation, and were ready to accompany their migrating masters, to be sold or captured along the way. Practically every dog name is based upon the geographic area from which that creature arrived. The spotted dog, for example,

may not have originated in Dalmatia (it was India, in fact), but it came through there and that was good enough for its new owners. So, too, with the spaniel (allegedly *espagnol*), the greyhound (allegedly Greek), the saluki (thought to be Seleucid).

With the Age of Discovery, mankind's hitherto slow movements were transformed. No longer did small groups wander along conventional lines; instead, boatloads leapfrogged between the continents. Everyone took dogs along with them and brought dogs back. There was much panmixia, or wide-scale interbreeding. Sometimes this was successful; sometimes not. New breeds were developed, often at the expense of the native varieties that died out, as in America and South Africa.

At this stage the human comparison becomes intense. Native human breeds have been extinguished; think of Tasmania, of South America. And there has been interbreeding, creating new varieties and colors of men; think of the West Indies, of South Africa, of Hawaii. With dogs, the wish to preserve and intensify certain characteristics has been pursued vigorously. There have been some ghastly errors, such as overlong dogs whose abdomens trail on the ground; but in the main breeders have produced what they consider to be desirable characteristics.

Since, therefore, the history of dogs has many parallels to our own, it is worthwhile spending a little time on it in order to probe, perhaps, into our own future. The Canidae were derived—fairly recently, in the late Pliocene and early Pleistocene epochs—from more primitive predators. Among the Canidae was the wolf (*Canis lupus*), a species having much in common with early man, for each exhibited co-operative be-

havior when attacking its prey. Wolf and man were direct competitors, and this similarity of life style may have had much to do with their eventual union. It is believed that all modern dogs derive only from the various subspecies of *Canis lupus* and that the association of wolf and man that led to dog happened again and again: American Indians frequently captured wolf cubs, either to amend their dog stock or to start afresh. This process of turning wolves into dogs was probably spurred on by the considerable growth of forest at the end of the Ice Age, when man's extreme inability to smell out his prey in that tangle of hiding places became a terrible disadvantage.

Anyway, the dog, a remarkable social invention, was the first domestic animal. (Some say it was the reindeer, but it is difficult to exploit reindeer without the aid of dogs.) Man's new accomplice could be tamed, if caught early enough and reared in human company. It could hunt. It could herd animals. It could protect and give warning, although wild Canidae are not as given to protective barking as the tame varieties are.

However, a good forest dog is not necessarily suitable for open plains, or for herding semidomestic stocks, or for guarding encampments. Therefore, there had to be selective breeding for specific purposes. This is thought to have occurred primarily during the Paleolithic and Mesolithic ages, or between twenty thousand and ten thousand years ago. Recognizably different breeds of dog have been recovered from archaeological sites of that time, notably in more northerly regions, and by the time the Mesolithic was yielding to the Neolithic there were hunting dogs, sheep dogs, and even toy dogs of the Maltese type. At least five major kinds

In Pompeii, Cave canem

Fourteenth-century acrobats

Miss Bowles, by Reynolds

lived with the early Egyptians: the basenji, the greyhound, the Maltese, the mastiff, and a sort of chow.

It is important to appreciate that the changes, however striking, were not basic. They were more of degree. For example, take an ordinary dog of average proportions and place it in front of a set of distorting mirrors. Though the dog may bark with instant disquietude, it is possible to make it look whippet-thin, or spitz-faced, or as massive as a mastiff. Of course, dogs also differ in those characteristics that were different even among wolves, such as color, temperament, or the wiriness, smoothness, or furriness of hair. With man, too, there is great variability, either unsuppressed or strengthened by natural selection, in such things as hair and personality.

A large number of the differences in dogs are the result of neoteny, the retention of juvenile features. This process occurs when a creature stops growing or achieves its adult state while still possessing characteristics previously associated with its more immature form. Puppies, for example, have silkier, less wiry hair. Their ears, in general, are floppier than those of the adult, and their tails are more likely to droop. There is no law that these features must be linked with the juvenile form, but some of the changes in dogs have inclined toward these puppy-like features. (Many of the Pekinese characteristics are an example.) Human beings are also believed to demonstrate some neoteny: their skin is thought to be smoother and more baby-like than before; their general hairiness reduced; their supraorbital ridges, those bony eyebrows that characterized early man, less pronounced.

Just as Neolithic man's dog requirements differed from place to place, so modern breeders have had to adapt their stock to the environment. The big mastiffs have been made yet bigger, and built for war. Pet and toy breeds, suitable for living within a household, have become more favored. In the Aztec world, dogs were bred for eating, for their hair, and as beasts of burden. The whiteness of the English terriers was needed for greater conspicuousness within the undergrowth. Even the arrival of breech-loading guns demanded a different animal: the steadfast and patient behavior of the pointer, doggedly stationary while his master fulfilled the ritual of preparing a muzzleloader, was far too steadfast when a more capable firing piece became available. Therefore, setters were deliberately bred from spaniel stock to sit, or "set," when the quarry was detected and then move forward when the quicker gun was ready.

Breeders, whether by putting their animals out at night to mate with wolves or actively preventing such an event, or by trading particular animals up and down the migration routes, have always attempted to satisfy particular needs. During the past twenty thousand years, these men have been outstandingly successful in unleashing the potential variation in the domestic dog, the animal that was once the wolf.

Not only have physical characteristics been a consideration; behavior has also been important. The breeder has had to concern himself with an animal's ferocity (guard dogs), or overall friendliness (general pets), or individual friendliness (loyalty to one person alone). There is, for example, the matter of barking. Some individual dogs bark more than others; some breeds do. It can even be proved, and Scott and Fuller have done so, that this trait has a genetic basis.

For their experiment, they took the basenji, a poor barker, and the cocker spaniel, a noisier creature. Basenjis not only bark rarely, but make less noise when they do and stop more quickly should they start. Presumably, barking served less purpose in the African forests, or was pounced on more readily by dog-loving leopards. Whether their masters selected them for their quietness, or whether leopards saved them the trouble, the modern examples of this African breed howl more than they bark. Any kind of howl, with its wavering note, is harder to pinpoint than a bark. The cocker, on the other hand, named for its ability to flush out woodcock, is a barker. Prompted to do so, cockers barked 68 per cent of the time during the experiment. Basenjis not only barked less loudly and more briefly when given similar stimuli, but responded only 20 per cent of the time.

This behavioral characteristic, bark-a-lot versus bark-a-little, was therefore a most suitable trait for investigation. The experimenters' plan was to cross a cocker with a basenji, to cross again the offspring of this mixed mating, and then to backcross the second generation both with pure cockers and with pure basenjis. At each stage the willingness to bark would be noted.

The eventual result of all this breeding, and of all its measured noise, was clear. Whereas pure cockers barked, as already mentioned, at 68 per cent of the stimuli, the basenji-cocker crosses barked at only 60 per cent of similar provocations. By the time the offspring had been crossed with each other, the willingness to bark had been reduced to 55 per cent. But then came the backcrosses. When the second generation (of mixed basenji-cocker stock) was mated with pure cockers, the result was a 65 per cent proneness to bark. The other

Freud, with obsession

Disney's Pluto

"He's in love with a Basset who moved away."

Thurber's faithful friend

backcross (with pure basenjis) resulted only in a 50 per cent response. In other words, genetic inheritance plays a crucial role in this type of behavior.

Human beings also have such behavioral traits, whether as individuals or as groups, and these too are sometimes genetically based. (For a time it was frequently stated that heredity had no effect on human behavior, but this was during a period of widespread revulsion against the exaggerated claims of the early eugenicists.) Which language we speak is, of course, environmental, but the latent ability to speak is genetic. Therefore, although it may be simplest to think of genetic traits in terms of physical characteristics—height, eye color, limb shape and proportion—it should never be forgotten that personality, manner, and other features of our behavior are just as involved. It is possibly more comforting to imagine that our own individuality has come to us in some mystic manner outside the normal laws, but it has done nothing of the kind. It is as genetically based as the rest of us.

It is not impossible to imagine that mankind may one day apply its enthusiasm for breeding to humanity itself. Biological advance and greater genetic knowledge will steadily make it easier for him to do so. But as of now, the tendency toward diversity has gone to greater lengths in the dog than in man, and for two reasons. First, natural selection for the dog has been relaxed for a longer time—in terms of generations— than for man. Second, artificial selection of the dog by man has deliberately preserved some unwelcome canine mutations merely to increase that diversity. Has the dog species therefore suffered genetically? Natural selection is impartial, favoring no species in particular, but has its lack of influence caused some

kind of discernible unfitness in the dog?

The answer is that the dog does not seem to be genetically weak. For example, current breeds are generally more fertile than their wolf ancestors. Wolves mature at the age of two, and produce four or five cubs per annual litter. There may be selective reasons for this casual growth, such as the inability of the habitat to support large numbers of predators, but the wolf is relatively infertile. The dog is usually mature sexually before the age of one and can produce two litters a year. By this criterion, man-handling has not harmed it.

Nor has it reduced the range of its capabilities. As with human beings, variety is the keynote, and today's dogs have broadened the old wolf characteristics. Terriers, to quote Scott and Fuller again, are more aggressive than their wolf forebears; the hound breeds are less so. Greyhounds are faster than wolves; short-legged dogs, like the dachshund, are less so. Good scent-dogs are better trackers than wolves, while terriers are poorer. Sheep dogs can herd more effectively; other breeds would not know where to begin (think, very briefly, of the Pekinese).

Significantly, however, there is no dog that exceeds the wolf in every degree. Each dog ability has been achieved at the expense of some other virtue. (The ever-steady sense fixation of the bloodhound, for example, makes one fear, possibly, for his intelligence.) The various losses are important, for it is doubtful if any breed of dog could survive in a wilderness where it had to compete with the wolf.

In fact, dogs have become wild only where there is no such rivalry, as on the Australian continent. The aborigines arrived in that empty land during the Mesolithic Age, and are thought to have

brought the dingoes with them, either tamed as part of the community or semi-parasitic on its fringes. On that continent there had been a marsupial wolf, *Thylacynus,* surviving poorly in the forests, but the subsequent arrival of the white man helped put an end to its modest viability. The result of both events, of both white man and black invading the brown landscape, is that the yellow dog dingo is now wild and howling at the moon. The dingo's attributes are more general than specialized, and it has made effective use of all of them in conquering the continent.

Natural selection does not, then, favor the creation of some superbeast, highly able in every degree. Either the result is a good all-rounder like the wolf, able to track, scent, co-operate, and run, or a specialist, closely adapted to the needs of some precise habitat. Man took the all-rounder wolf and turned it into a whole range of dog specialists, each excellent in something but always paying the price by losing something else.

This same rule probably applies in no smaller degree to humans. All those mythical Greek heroes were strong *and* cunning *and* beautiful *and* fertile *and* wise. The more down-to-earth story of the dog teaches us something quite different. Only society can be superhuman, as wide-ranging as the variability within it, as excellent as all the peaks of brilliance within its compass. To breed wisely, therefore, would necessarily be to treasure the variation. It would not be, as Heinrich Himmler wrongly supposed, to choose a particular ideal and aim for that alone.

Anthony Smith is an English free-lance writer. This article is adapted from his latest book, The Human Pedigree, *to be published this April by J. B. Lippincott.*

Loyal Lassie

Snoopy cavorting

THE LURE OF
THE
VIKINGS

Odin, deity of wisdom and war and supreme god of the Vikings, rides to battle in the relief above. One of his worshipers carved the awesome face opposite as decoration for the frame of a wooden cart.

W ere they,

as one contemporary claimed, "the filthiest people

under God"? Perhaps

—but from Icelandic saga to present-day comic strip,

an aura of romance surrounds them

By LIONEL CASSON

"Came three ships of Northmen. . . . And then the reve [sheriff] rode to the place, and would have driven them to the king's residence, because he knew not who they were: and they slew him. These were the first ships of Danishmen which sought the land of the English nation."

So wrote the compiler of the Anglo-Saxon Chronicle under the date 787. Six years later, as the entry for 793 records, "the ravaging of heathen men lamentably destroyed God's church at Lindisfarne through rapine and slaughter." Lindisfarne was an island off the coast of Northumbria near England's border with Scotland, and the site of a venerated monastic community. The "heathen men" were either Danes or Norwegians, and, by the time they left, most of the monks had been slaughtered or carried off for sale and the buildings looted and burned. The Age of the Vikings had opened.

The word "Viking" conjures up for most of us an image of vast, bearded hordes of blond or red-haired, horn-helmeted giants in long ships heading through northern mists for western lands unknown. They were blond and red-haired all right, but giants only by the standards of the day: the skeletons that have been uncovered show an average height of 5 feet 8 inches; the chieftain buried in the celebrated tomb at Gokstad in Norway was no more than 5 feet 6 inches. Furthermore, the dauntless venturers to the north were a relatively small group. Most of the Vikings—the bulk of the Norwegians and practically all of those from Denmark and Sweden—made their mark in history on land, well-civilized land at that, for it was there that the best markets for trade or targets for raids were found.

From roughly A.D. 800 to almost 1200, western Europe struggled ceaselessly to ward off the marauding bands of Danes and Norwegians. Since both the Danes and Norwegians were heathen for a good part of the period—the Danes were converted about the middle of the tenth century, the Norwegians not until a half century or so later

KING EDMUND'S FATE

Marauding Vikings from Denmark swept into England in about A.D. 870. Above, they storm a town, probably Thetford. Below, they drag the defeated King Edmund of East Anglia from his throne after he has unwisely scorned them as pagans. Edmund's troubles at the hands of the Vikings, as set forth in these miniatures from a twelfth-century English manuscript called "The Miracles of St. Edmund," scarcely ended with his dethronement. For what happened to him next, see opposite.

—the monasteries, convents, and churches were not only fair game but, being the richest institutions around, the preferred game. Summer after summer the Danes descended upon Holland and northern France, blazing a trail of destruction all the way to Paris. The Norwegians, moving farther down the coast, concentrated on the lower reaches of the Loire, while the two together swarmed over Brittany. For a while the harried inhabitants were able to breathe freely as they watched the long ships sail off to pass the winter back home, but they lost even that respite when the invaders discovered the convenience of wintering in France. This also allowed them to extend their range. In 844, for example, an adventurous pack of Vikings coasted along Portugal and Spain to capture Cádiz and Seville and even raid Córdoba before the Moors finally rallied and sent them limping home by the end of the year. In 859 another pack tried a return visit, found the coasts of Spain too closely guarded, and pushed on to pass the winter in south France. The next year, fully refreshed, they sailed to Italy and sacked Pisa.

It was not that the Vikings were invincible in battle. Their favored weapon, the battle-axe, had long been abandoned by less primitive nations, their swords were inferior to the Frankish swords (which Viking chieftains preferred to the local products), and they never got the hang of besieging a fortification. What made them so formidable were their superb ships and skilled seamanship. These gave them so total a command of the water that no force ever dared engage them there, and as a consequence they had unlimited mobility. They were able at will to make swift and sudden onslaughts and, if pressed, beat hasty and safe retreats.

In France, kings and local rulers, finding it too hard to drive the invaders off, tried to buy them off, offering them handsome sums to stay away. In time-honored fashion bribery soon became blackmail, the Danes in particular insisting on periodic payments—the notorious Danegeld. Some harassed lead-

Adding injury to insult, Vikings bind King Edmund, flog him, and drag him away. Later they used him as a target for archery practice and finally beheaded him. Ultimately he was raised to sainthood and his cult flourished at Bury St. Edmunds.

ers turned to using compliant Vikings as mercenaries to fight their brothers. Unfortunately, they had a nasty tendency to moonlight. In 862, for example, the count of Anjou hired some Viking bands settled in the Loire to give him a hand. The following year they turned around and burned the abbey of Saint Hilaire and held up the city of Poitiers for ransom. Eventually the kings of France, finding it impossible to lick them, decided to join them: in 911 Hrolfr—or Rollo, to give him the more pronounceable name he is better known by, who was either a Dane or a Norwegian—was made the first duke of Normandy, in other words, acknowledged ruler of the lands his Northmen actually held. It turned out to be an astute move on the part of Charles the Simple. Rollo stood by the king and helped him fend off other Vikings. Although his men hardly became well-behaved citizens overnight, time and marriage with local girls gradually changed them from raiding Northmen to settled Normans.

Across the Channel, England and Ireland were having even worse trouble. In 835 Danish Vikings appeared on the Thames, and from that time on they not only raided but held a large chunk of eastern England called the Danelaw (i.e., the region where Danish law prevailed). From 991 on, they regularly collected Danegeld to boot. The Norwegians, on the other hand, concentrated on northwest England and Ireland (they ruled practically all of it for half of the tenth century). Though the Norman Conquest in 1066 marked the beginning of the end for them as well as the Danes, they held out in a number of the islands. (In the Orkneys they stayed right up to 1468.)

The Danes and Norwegians, though active enough traders, preferred the pleasures of fighting and the quicker profits of plunder. The Swedes, on the other hand, were as much interested in trade as in fighting and found their best customers in the rich caliphate of Baghdad. As a result they were drawn deeper and deeper into Russia.

The Slavic population called the newcomers Rus—whence the name Russia. We think of Igor, Vladimir, Oleg, as typically Russian names. Not at all: Igor is a Slavic version of Ingmar, Vladimir of Valdemar, Oleg of Helge. As a matter of fact, many historians argue that it was Swedish Vikings who founded the first Russian state, although others, particularly Soviet historians, do not agree.

The Swedes furnished their Arab customers with furs and slaves; the first they garnered in the forests of their homeland, the second in the Slavic populations they passed through (thereby contributing to making "Slav" the origin of our word "slave"). As early as the closing years of the eighth century their long ships had nosed past the coasts of

A ship with furled sail adorns this silver Viking coin struck in A.D. 825 at Hedeby, a port on the Baltic-North Sea route where furs and ivories from the north were exchanged for the Rhineland's cloth and wine.

Finland, up the Baltic rivers in the East Russian plain, and then down the Volga. Here Turkish Bulgars and Khazars, who held the lands north of the Caspian, were the intermediaries in linking caravan routes to the market at Baghdad. Within fifty years the Swedes had worked out a different, shorter route farther west that eliminated any intermediaries and opened up the equally rich market at Constantinople. This route ran by way of lakes and rivers, with some portages, to the head of the Dnieper and then downriver to the Crimea on the Black Sea. From there it was but a short stretch along the

coast to the Bosporus and Constantinople. The rich capital was, in fact, so temptingly near that in 860 bands of Swedes decided to raid it. They had two hundred ships and the Byzantine army and navy happened to be away at the time, but even so the city's massive defense wall proved too much for them. Constantinople's rulers responded with typical Byzantine astuteness: they started a campaign to convert the heathens to Christianity. At the same time, they intrigued with the Khazars, the Swedes' neighbors to the southeast. It all worked so well that, a century later, a contingent of Swedes formed the imperial guard at Constantinople.

After 850 a significant political development began. A certain Rurik built up a powerful Viking state based in Novgorod, some 125 miles south of Leningrad and within easy reach of the Baltic. A decade later two other leaders, Askold and Dir, broke away from Novgorod to carve out a kingdom at Kiev (it was probably they who launched the abortive raid on Constantinople). Then, about 880, Rurik's son Oleg captured Kiev and put together a single state that controlled the whole of the trade route from the Gulf of Finland to the Black Sea. The land was, it is true, still owned by the Slavic aristocracy, but the rulers were the Swedes. Oleg's merger of miscellaneous Slavic tribes into a single political entity was, so far as we know, the first "Russian" state.

On June 21, 921, the caliph at Baghdad dispatched an embassy to the Bulgars living along the middle Volga, including as secretary an inquisitive and observant fellow named Ahmed Ibn Fadlan. The route took them through a community of Rus living along the Volga, and it occurred to Ibn Fadlan to note down his impressions. By great good luck his account has survived. What is more, since some chieftain had just died, it contains among other things a description of a full-scale Viking funeral. It is worth quoting at length:

"I saw the Rus who were there for commerce and come down the river Atul [the Volga]. I have never seen bodies

A snarling beast, carved in wood, sits atop what is thought to be a chair post. This masterpiece of Viking art, adorned with animal motifs and geometric patterns, was found early in this century at a Viking burial site in Oseberg, Norway.

69

плѣнъ рѹсскы

наждвъдръстрѣ

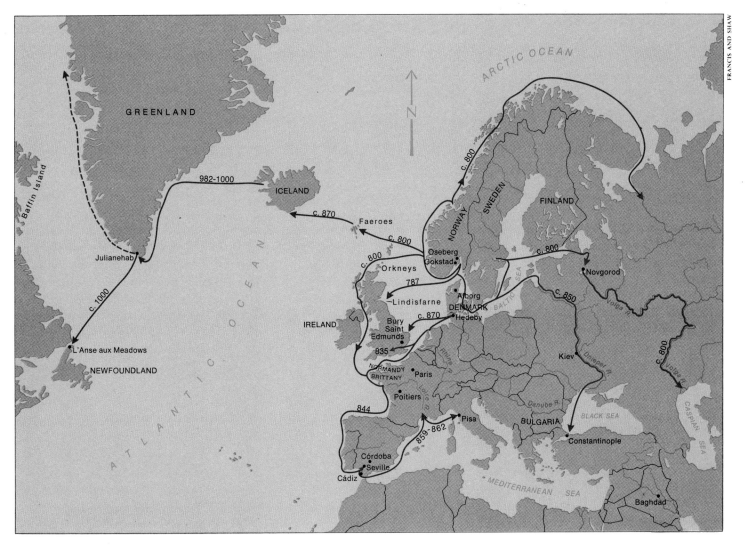

The map above shows the expanse of the Vikings' range—from the Volga River to the New World, from Gibraltar to the Arctic, an astonishing mileage record for their time.

more perfect than theirs. One would say they are as tall as palm trees. They are blonde and florid in complexion.... The men wear a garment that leaves one side of their body and one hand free. Everyone carries an axe, sword, and knife at all times.... From the tip of their nails to their neck their bodies are tattooed in green with designs of trees, figures, and the like....

"They are the filthiest people under god. They never wash off excrement or urine; they do not wash after sexual relations; they do not wash their hands after meals. They are like wild donkeys.

"When they arrive from their country they anchor their boats on the Atul, which is a mighty river, and build along its bank large wooden houses. In each one of these, ten and twenty people, more or less, live together. Each has a

bed on which he rests. With them are beautiful young female slaves intended for the slave merchants. Each of the men will have sexual relations with his slave with his companions looking on. Sometimes whole bunches of them unite in this manner, one in front of the other. If a slave merchant enters to buy a young slave from one of them and finds the master in the midst of having relations with her, the master does not withdraw from her before having satisfied his needs.

"Every day they must wash their face and head, and they do it in the dirtiest and filthiest way possible. Every morning the young serving girl arrives carrying a large bowl full of water. She puts it before her master, and he washes his hands and his face as well as his hair. He washes and combs out his hair into the basin, and then blows his nose and spits and does every other possible filthy act into this water. When he has finished what he has to do, the servant carries the bowl to the man next to him, and this

one does just as his companion had done. She continues to pass the bowl from one to the other till it has made the circle of all who live in the house....

"One of the customs of the king of the Rus is to have with him in his palace four hundred men who are the bravest of his companions and on whom he can count. These are men who die with him and commit suicide for him. With each is a young female slave who waits on him, washes his head, and prepares all his food and drink, and another female slave with whom he has relations. These four hundred men sit below the king's throne, which is enormous and encrusted with the finest precious stones. With the king sit forty female slaves destined for his bed. It can happen that he will have relations with one of them in the presence of his companions whom we have just mentioned without getting off the throne. When he has to take care of bodily needs, he does it in a basin. If he wants to get on his horse, they lead his horse right to the throne and he

Svyatoslav, prince of Novgorod, was third in the Norse dynasty that ruled Russia. Here, in a fourteenth-century Slavic manuscript illumination, he rides forth on a white horse, top center, to make war on the fierce Bulgars about A.D. 965.

mounts from there. If he wants to get off his horse, he makes it go up so that he can get off right onto the throne. . . ."

The *pièce de résistance* during his stay there was the grandiose funeral:

"I was told that, for their important personages, in case of death they do certain things of which cremation is the least. I wanted to know for certain about this, and I was able when I heard that a man of considerable importance among them had died. . . . When a great personage dies, the members of his family say to his female and male slaves, 'Which of you will die with him?' One of them says, 'I.' Once he or she has said that, it becomes obligatory, it is impossible to turn back. . . . Most of the time it is the female slaves who do it. . . . She is entrusted to two other young female slaves who watch over her and who are with her wherever she goes, to the point of at times washing her feet with their own hands. People busy themselves about the corpse to cut clothing for it and prepare everything that is necessary. Every day during this period the female slave drinks and sings, giving herself over to joy and gaiety. . . .

"When the day arrived for the deceased to be cremated and the girl with him, I went to the river where his boat was. I saw that they had pulled the boat up on the bank, had set up four stakes of various kinds of wood for it, and that around these stakes they had set up sort of great scaffolds of wood. Then they drew the boat so that it was set upon this framework of wood. . . .

"Then they brought a bed, placed it [in a tent] on the boat, and covered it with a spread of Greek brocade and cushions of the same brocade. Then came an old woman whom they call the Angel of Death and it was she who

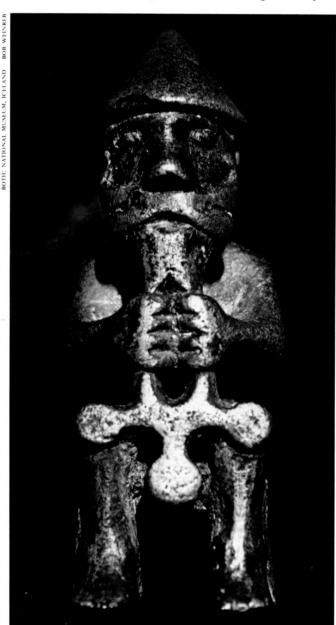

This bronze figure is very likely Thor, the quick-tempered god of thunder. He is gripping what appears to be a three-headed hammer.

spread the furnishings just mentioned on the bed. She is the one in charge of sewing and arranging all that, and it is she who kills the young slaves. . . .

"I saw that the corpse had turned black because of the cold. . . . It did not smell bad and nothing about it had changed except its color. They dressed it in pants, hose, boots, a tunic, and a caftan of brocade with gold buttons. They put on as headdress a cap of brocade covered with sable. Then they carried it and brought it inside the tent that was on the boat, set it on the bedspread, and propped it up with cushions. Then they

brought beer, fruits, and aromatic plants which they placed by it. Then they brought bread, meat, and onions which they cut in two and threw beside it. Then they took two horses, ran them until they were in a sweat, cut them into pieces with blows of the sword, and threw their flesh into the boat. Next they led up two cows which they cut into pieces in the same way and also threw into the boat. Next they brought a cock and a chicken, killed them, and threw them into the boat.

"Meanwhile the slave girl who wanted to be killed went back and forth, entering in turn each of a series of tents [that had been put up], and the master of each tent had sexual relations with her. And he said, 'Tell your master that I did this only out of love for him.' . . .

"They led her to the boat. She took off the two bracelets that she had on and gave them both to the old woman who was called the Angel of Death, the one who does the killing. Then she took off her two ankle bracelets and gave them to the two young girls who had attended her and were the daughters of the woman called the Angel of Death. Then they made her get up on the boat but without going into the tent. Then men came with shields and clubs. She was handed a cup of beer. She uttered a chant in taking it and drank it. My interpreter tells me that she was thus saying farewell to all her companions. Then someone brought another cup, she took it and sang for a long time until the old woman urged her to drink up and pressed her to enter the tent in which her master was.

"I saw that the young girl was bewildered. She wanted to go into the tent, but she put her head between the tent and the boat. Then the old woman seized her by the head and made her go

into the tent and entered along with her. Then the men set about beating with their clubs on their shields so that no one would hear the sound of her cries and other slave girls would not be frightened and would not try to escape death with their masters. Next six men entered the tent and had relations with the young girl. Next they laid her down beside her master. Two seized her two feet, two others her hands. The old woman called the Angel of Death came up, put a cord about her neck so that the two ends were apart and gave it to two men to pull. Then she went up to the girl, holding a dagger with a wide blade, and kept plunging it between the ribs and pulling it out while the two men strangled with the cord until the girl was dead.

"Then the nearest of kin to the deceased, after they had placed the young girl who had been killed at the side of her master, came, took a piece of wood that he had ignited and, walking backwards, with the back of his head toward the boat and his face toward the people, one hand holding the lighted brand and the other covering his anus— for he was completely nude—went up to set fire to the wood that had been put under the boat. Then people came up with brands and more wood to burn, each one holding a brand aflame at the tip and which he threw on the wood heaped under the boat. The fire swept over the wood, then the boat, then the tent, the corpse, the girl and all that was on the boat."

We can see through Ibn Fadlan's observant eye that the Rus he was among were showing signs of assimilation. They were, of course, still very much Swedish Vikings, carrying their traditional weapons, maintaining barbaric standards of hygiene, and incinerating their dead in the approved style. But they had learned to cover their beds with Greek brocades, to wear the caftan for ceremonial occasions, and to load their women with jewelry in Oriental fashion. Their leaders had, moreover, discovered

TEXT CONTINUED ON PAGE 77

Viking foot soldiers strode into battle brandishing swords such as the double-edged weapon with inlaid pommel at right. Often passed down from father to son, the swords were given suitably militant names like Gleam of Battle and Thorn of the Shields.

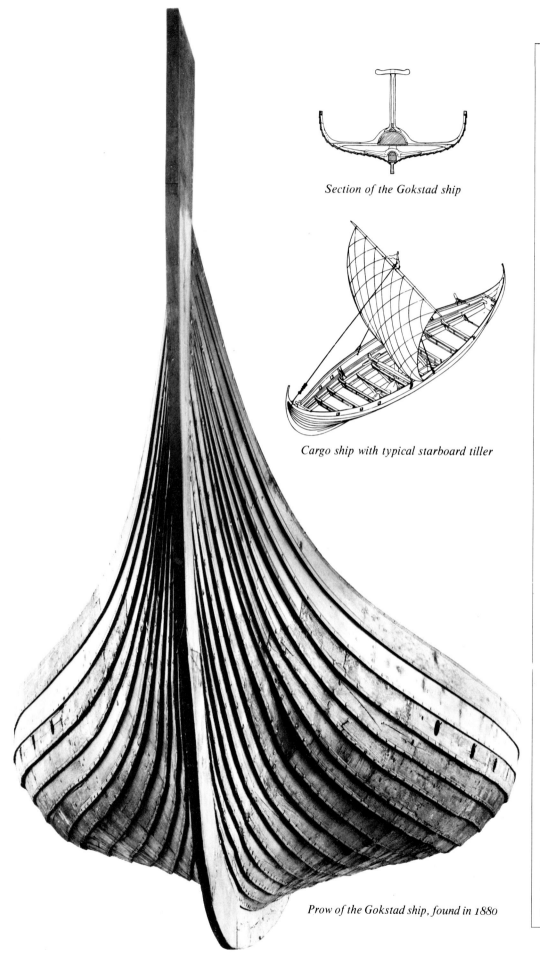

Section of the Gokstad ship

Cargo ship with typical starboard tiller

Prow of the Gokstad ship, found in 1880

A TALE OF TWO SHIPS

Above all else, it was their magnificent ships that enabled the Vikings to dominate the Western world from Vinland to Byzantium. It is not surprising, therefore, that many a Viking chose to be buried in a ship. Two particularly well-preserved ship burials (as archaeologists call them), both unearthed in Norway, have given us a wealth of knowledge about Viking ways on land and sea.

The ship at far left was found in 1880 under a mound of earth at the sea's edge in Gokstad. In it, a Viking chieftain was laid reverently to rest in a timbered chamber in the stern. Nothing better displays the prodigious skill of Viking seamen and shipwrights than the Gokstad vessel. Once capable of long ocean voyages, it is seventy-eight feet long, sixteen feet in beam, and constructed of sturdy oak. Like most Viking ships, it is double-ended and clinker-built (that is, with overlapping planks, like house siding), and it has a single steering oar attached to a tiller so ingeniously rigged as to be easily manageable even in the heaviest weather. Ingeniously, too, the Gokstad ship was provided with thirty-two pivoted shutters that sealed the oarports against the waves. (Now restored, the vessel is on view at the Viking Museum in Oslo.)

Like the Gokstad ship, the ship opposite, discovered at Oseberg in 1903, had been looted long before its rediscovery. Robbers had, among other things, broken off its prow, which rose fifteen feet upward to end in a dragon's head. Nonetheless, enough carvings remained to hint at the richness of the artifacts that were buried with the bodies of the two women—a highborn young lady and her elderly servant—who were entombed in the ship. Besides the human and animal heads on pages 65 and 68, and the frieze of frenzied, twining animals that outlines the bow opposite, the tomb contained a handsomely carved four-wheeled cart, sledges for winter travel, beds, tents, looms, and all manner of domestic comforts—virtually everything the departed could possibly want.

Throughout Scandinavia thousands of such ship burials have been found. In death as in life, it would seem, the noblest and most enduring symbols of Viking strength and power are ships like these.

The Oseberg ship emerges from the earth, 1903

the delights of a harem. As time went on, they increasingly picked up the customs of their new home, until eventually they were submerged in the sea of peoples about them.

Unfortunately, we have no such reports on the Vikings in the West. There we have to depend largely on the accounts of clerics, who vouchsafe only a few statements on the Viking way of life as they expatiate on Viking destructiveness. There is, however, one other important source of information—the stories the Vikings tell about themselves, the sagas of such heroes as Eric the Red, his son Leif, Oleg Tryggvason, and other mighty mariners and brandishers of the battle-axe. It is these that have not only given rise to our stereotype of the Vikings but also record their discovery of the New World.

All the Vikings were expert seamen, but the Norwegians, living in a land whose coast was lined with excellent harbors that faced the open sea, were the most skilled and daring. For their voyages they developed the robust, graceful galleys that we know so well from the three Viking tombs uncovered between 1867 and 1903. In such ships Viking seafarers had by 800 made their way to the Faroe Islands, and within a century thereafter established themselves firmly in Iceland. And around 900 a certain Gunbjørn, en route from Norway to Iceland, was blown so far past his destination that he caught sight of the coast of Greenland.

An actual landing on Greenland had to wait almost one hundred years. It was then, in the year 982, that the celebrated Eric the Red appeared on the scene. A Norwegian who had settled in Iceland, Eric was banished for three years for committing murder and decided to spend the time looking for the land Gunbjørn had seen so long ago. With a boatload of family and kindred spirits he managed to get to the southwest

coast of Greenland, the less formidable part, and there he set up camp and spent the three winters of his exile. Finally free to return to Iceland, he collected recruits for a colony on Greenland (as he glibly dubbed the new country in order to make it sound more attractive), and sailed off, his fleet of twenty-five ships filled with men and their families and animals. The journey was so hard that, of the twenty-five ships, only fourteen came through, but it was enough to start a permanent settlement near what is today called Julianehab. Danish archaeologists excavating the site have, in fact,

Two stylized gold dragons are entwined in each other's coils in the pattern of this typical brooch from the late Viking period.

found Eric's very house, a typical Viking "long house" whose great central room, which served as kitchen and bedroom as well as living room, was 49 feet long and 15 feet wide and whose walls were of solid earth 10 feet thick.

Eric's more famous son, Leif, the man who was to complete this chapter of Viking history, started as a missionary. He left Greenland for Norway, became a Christian there, and was finally sent home to convert his father's colony. But his heart was never really in it, particularly since his father took a dim view of the project. By about the year 1000 he had given up proselytizing and turned to

exploring. Some years earlier, he knew, Gunbjørn's experience had been repeated: a boat going from Iceland to Greenland had been carried clean past it to unknown shores, and the captain had reported that he had sighted land three times, a well-wooded coast twice, and once a rocky, ice-bound island. Leif, fascinated by the story, ultimately bought the same boat and with a party of thirty-five set out to investigate. He came upon the rocky island easily enough, then a wooded area, and, two days later, an island with abundant grass. They landed on the mainland opposite, where there was plenty of timber for building huts, where rivers and sea teemed with the biggest salmon they had ever seen, where there were no frosts in winter and grass was green almost all year round, and where day and night were of far more equal duration than in Greenland or Iceland.

While reconnoitering the area, they hit upon the most surprising find of all—vines bearing grapes. This so impressed Leif that he called the place "Wineland," or, to give it the form we commonly use, Vinland. Leif and company wintered there and sailed home in the spring. Sometime later, Leif's brother Torwald went to Vinland, found Leif's abandoned huts, and spent two years looking around —only to be killed by an arrow in a scuffle with a great number of natives in skin boats. In the following years, yet two more expeditions reached the new land.

These events, we must keep in mind, are not told in archival documents or even contemporary chronicles but in poems chanted by Icelandic bards centuries after they had taken place. How much, then, is history and how much poetic imagination?

The consensus has always been that the sagas have a core of solid fact, that Vikings actually did get to the New World and establish some sort of settlement there. A Danish archaeological

At the top of this carved stone monument from Sweden is a mythological scene: it may represent the arrival in Valhalla of Odin astride his eight-legged horse, Sleipnir. Below is a double-ended warship and its well-armed crew.

77

team, conducting excavations from 1961 to 1968 at L'Anse aux Meadows in the northernmost tip of Newfoundland, put it beyond doubt. They unearthed the remains of houses and boat sheds, a bronze ring-headed pin and other material, all of it unquestionably Norse and datable to about 1000. No one, however, will go so far as to suggest that these are the actual remains of Leif's own expedition, or that northern Newfoundland is indeed Vinland. On the contrary, the site of this fabled land—green almost all year around, with abundant forests and rivers teeming with salmon, inhabited by natives using skin boats, and, above all, bearing grapes in profusion—has provoked nearly as much argument and theorizing as the lost Atlantis.

The conservative-minded prefer to place Vinland as near Greenland as possible, in Baffin Island or its vicinity. Such regions are, of course, hardly green all year around and produce as many grapes as frogs do feathers, but these and similar stumbling blocks can always be dismissed as mere bardic embroidery. (The most recent voice for this school argues that the shore was across the straits from Baffin Island and gets around the grapes by arguing that "Wineland" really means "pastureland.")

The less conservative have offered locations as far south as Virginia. Many submit in evidence a round tower at Newport, Rhode Island, which, they stoutly assert, shows unmistakable marks of Viking workmanship. Others assert, equally stoutly, and with more reason, that it shows unmistakable marks of workmanship no earlier than colonial times.

Then there is the notorious Kensington Stone, which a few use to argue for Viking penetration as far as the Midwest. The stone, complete with a perfectly preserved inscription in runic script, the standard Viking writing, turned up on a farm near Kensington, Minnesota. The owner delivered it to the local bank to put on display and, when it was handed back to him as a forgery, dumped it in his backyard where

he used it for a step. Along came a certain Hjalmar R. Holand; he was interested in it. The farmer gave it to him, and he spent the next fifty years passionately defending its authenticity. In addition to the stone, Holand had other Viking artifacts to offer—four axes, a battle-axe, some swords, and three rather light halberds. Unfortunately, none of the artifacts had been found *in situ,* and the halberds turned out to be not halberds at all but tobacco cutters

Archaeologists dig at L'Anse aux Meadows in northern Newfoundland, where the Vikings founded a settlement in about A.D. *1000.*

made in the last century by the Rogers Iron Company of Springfield, Ohio, to advertise the American Tobacco Company's Battle Axe Plug Tobacco. Until a less suspicious inscription turns up, or some real halberds or other conclusive form of evidence, we must simply admit that we do not know where Leif's Vinland was. (The celebrated Vinland map never shed much light on the question either—even before Yale University, in 1974, reluctantly declared it to be a forgery.)

The fortunes of the Viking settlements in North America parallel the fortunes of the Vikings' appearance in

history: they make a spectacular entrance upon the scene, hold the center of the stage for a while, and then retreat into the background, leaving scant trace of the starring role they had once played. In England, their long years of occupation left little more in the way of tangible traces than some local place names and some influences upon English law. In France, only some place names are left: feudalism and Christianity combined to strip the Vikings of their individuality and assimilate them into the peoples living around them. In Russia, they left nothing permanent except the country's name. Even in Greenland their settlements gradually petered out and the island had to be rediscovered in the sixteenth century.

But the Viking legend—that is made of far sterner stuff. In 1893 Magnus Andersen of Norway sailed a replica of the Gokstad ship across the Atlantic to help celebrate the World Columbian Exposition. In the 1950's Frans Bengtsson's novel *The Long Ships,* which portrayed Vikings with about the same degree of verisimilitude a Western does cowboys, became a best seller and inevitably a movie, which, with Hollywood finickiness, boasted three exact copies of the Gokstad ship. Robert Marx, celebrated for snooping out sunken treasure and for other marine exploits, got the film company to give him one so he could satisfy a yen to cross the ocean as Leif had (he had already done it in a replica of Columbus's *Niña*). He shoved off in March of 1964 but before he got very far his craft ungallantly came apart—it had been put together with twentieth-century nails and not Viking joinery. In proper Viking style, therefore, he soused it with diesel oil and sent it blazing to its rest. And right now the doings of Hagar, a comic-strip Viking, enliven the funnies in many a daily newspaper. In the hearts of romantics and those who guide our various communication arts, the Vikings live as lustily as ever.

Lionel Casson is a professor of classics at New York University. He wrote "The Maverick Pharaoh" for the Summer, 1974, issue.

Some seven hundred Viking graves have been discovered in a cemetery near A borg, Denmark. Stones marking some of the graves outline the shapes of ship.

BARGES ON THE STOUR, circa 1811. *Moments before a summer squall, Constable sketched a darkening sky over the river near his home in Suffolk. "The ba*

e Stour . . . ," he wrote, "made me a painter and I am grateful."

"The Perfect Interpreter of the English Countryside"

John Constable in a self-portrait, 1806.

*J*ohn Constable
sought to paint the skies and trees and,
most of all, the light
of England—an idea that shocked the art
establishment of his time

By RONALD BLYTHE

Great artists are often seen as people who have been forced to struggle against enormous disadvantages in early life. John Constable is one artist who had no such struggle.

He was born at East Bergholt, Suffolk, in June of 1776, the second son of Golding and Ann Constable. The Constable family had farmed in the Stour Valley for generations and had gradually acquired more property downstream until, at the time of John's birth, they owned a prosperous string of mills and were among the leading agricultural merchants in the river trade. The business was so successful by the 1770's that Golding Constable was able to give up living in the hollow at Flatford Mill and build a "mansion house" in the village. The Stour villages—East Bergholt, Dedham, Stratford, Stoke, Nayland, and Bures—are fine towns full of magnificent architecture from the days of the medieval wool merchants, and during John Constable's boyhood they were being expanded by the Georgian gentry. These crucial years of the eighteenth century, which the artist could barely recall but which molded the character of nearly all the people he knew, have been described by agricultural historians as the golden years of English farming. For John Constable, the essence of this glorious scene had been set down in paint by Thomas Gainsborough.

There was, to Constable, something overwhelming in the fact that Gainsborough had once walked the lanes that he now strolled in his slow, deliberate, country fashion. He saw Gainsborough "in every hedge and hollow tree," and soon, scarcely daring to think about the consequences, he too was making up his mind to become an artist. "For long I foundered in the path and tottered on the threshold," he wrote, "and there never was any young man nearer being lost than myself." This was certainly a boyish self-dramatization, for when we see what actually happened to John Constable (once he had convinced his practical East Anglian parents that neither the church nor the flourishing fam-

ily business was for him), we will find that he was shown "the path" by some of the most helpful guides anyone could wish for. What was even more extraordinary, these people were living, as it were, on his very doorstep.

Although his advantages were remarkable, John Constable, a man whose favorite word was "placid," had been born into a world of violence and change. The American, French, and Industrial revolutions all occurred during his lifetime. And he himself, while seeking to prove the spiritual harmony of the natural universe, would be too revolutionary a painter to be understood.

But it was only where his painting was concerned that Constable was a revolutionary. In nearly every other way he was a conventional Tory gentleman who believed that the land is the source of all the best things in life, a God-given commodity that the landowners had to revere. The farmers worked for the landowners and the villagers worked for the farmers. It was all part of a divine pattern. His long and bitter struggle to be accepted as an artist by everyone, from the inhabitants of Suffolk to the members of the Royal Academy, was a wish to be an accepted part of the civilized world he so strongly believed in. His difficulties—and ultimate triumph—stemmed from his refusal to give the public what it wanted as the price for easy entry into that world.

"Painting," he said, "is a science, and should be pursued as an enquiry into the laws of nature." But the public did not want painting to be a science; they wanted painting to be a kind of magic. They did not want straightforward descriptions of the countryside they knew so well; they wanted stories and mystery in paint. They wanted to look into a picture as they could look into Virgil or into one of their favorite poems, *The Seasons,* and see an idealized existence. Constable bewildered—and annoyed—them by leaving out these literary and emotional references and painting instead the natural realities of a certain place at a certain moment. This now seems a reasonable thing to

do, but when Constable, at the very beginning of his career, confessed to his friend John Dunthorne that he intended to be a "natural painter," one of those rare peaks of total originality in art came into view.

Dunthorne was six years older than Constable and lived nearby in East Bergholt. He was one of those "odd men out" that so many villages produce, a plumber-glazier who was also an artist and a freethinker. Constable was still a boy when Dunthorne taught him to grind colors and encouraged him to sketch. The association between the miller's rather dandified son and the "atheist," as Dunthorne was called, was disapproved of in some quarters, though Golding Constable seems to have found it amusing. To him they were "Don Quixote and his Man Friday." "I shall endeavor to get a pure and unaffected manner of representing the scenes," his son confided to Dunthorne. "Nature is the fountain's head." And, every evening after work at the mill office, he carried sketchbook or easel into the fields and painted until the light failed.

In 1796, when he was twenty, Constable met J. T. Smith, an antiquary who encouraged him to make drawings of old cottages in the Stour villages. These beautiful little pencil sketches were made in a book small enough to be held in the palm of the hand, and Constable acquired a habit that he would have for the rest of his life. William Blake was amazed by the perfection of these sketchbooks. "Why, this is not drawing, but *inspiration,*" he told Constable. "I meant it for drawing," replied Constable in the sharp way that was to unnerve so many of his fellow artists.

How far this good-looking, steely, and, at the same time, deeply spiritual youth had to go in order to persuade his parents to let him study painting is not known. But in 1799 he left Suffolk with an annual allowance of one hundred pounds from his father and a student's pass for the school set up by the Royal Academy. Three years later, in 1802, Constable returned to Suffolk, trained

The artist's mother, c. 1810   *The artist's father, 1815*

Haunted all his life by the self-doubts of a relentless perfectionist, Constable relied heavily on his family and sympathetic friends. His parents' devotion eased the obscurity of his early years as a painter. "Pray take care of yourself, and . . . keep a good fire," urged his mother, Ann. "Be of good cheer John," wrote Golding Constable, "as in me you will find a parent & a sincere friend." Constable fondly recorded their features and the flower garden of their home in the paintings above and at right.

GOLDING CONSTABLE'S FLOWER GARDEN, *painted by the artist circa 1812-16*

and expecting to earn a living. His first step was to buy a cottage-studio away from his parents' house; his second, to find some sort of answer to the barrage of criticism that now began to pursue him. Inevitably, the trouble had started in his own family; with typical Suffolk common sense, they thought that he should provide the neighborhood with what it required—namely, portraits. Constable was willing to do them, but his rough, impressionistic brushwork was an immediate cause for complaint. His rich uncle, David Watts, summed up the general feeling when he advised Constable to "Paint a little starling on your easel with the words, 'Finish! Finish!'"

One neighbor, a Mr. Reade, did commission a painting of his house, and *Old Hall* was the first of what Constable called his "house portraits," the most superb of which is *Malvern Hall*, painted in 1810. Constable asked ten guineas for *Old Hall*; with *Malvern Hall* he would ask the world to see a new vision of art.

But in 1802 it was still Thomas Gainsborough and the old vision that enthralled him, and his great problem was reconciling the traditional landscape, which in many ways he admired and respected, with the "natural" truths he saw whenever he glanced out the window at Flatford Mill or looked across

the water meadows to Dedham. One thing he never worried about was finding a subject. His home valley, a six-mile stretch of East Anglian river scenery with church towers, huge trees, industrial buildings, and brilliant light, was an incomparable challenge. Later he would say he never wanted to paint any scene where he was not a "welcome guest." And, when the time came for him to show people what kind of artist he intended to be, he would choose the valley he knew so well as the subject for his first big picture.

*I*n *Dedham Vale* (1802), Constable looks through Gainsborough to the old seventeenth-century masters of landscape. The painting is also evidence that Constable had formed an influential new friendship, for its composition is remarkably like that of an exquisite seventeenth-century work by Claude Lorraine entitled *Hagar and the Angel.*

Sir George Beaumont owned this painting and was so fond of it that he had it hung in his carriage when he traveled. His mother lived in Dedham, and it was inevitable that the man who was about to be the greatest patron of the

Romantic movement and the man who was to be its leading painter should meet. It was an important friendship, for Sir George—whose collection would be the nucleus of the National Gallery he helped found—introduced Constable to the Rubens landscape called *Château de Steen,* to the paintings of other Flemish masters, and to the work of such "modern" artists as Thomas Girtin. When Sir George asked one day whose style he would choose for his own, Girtin's or the old masters', Constable replied that it would be neither. His, he said, would be "God Almighty's style."

Dr. Johnson once said, "We all know what light is, but it is not easy to *tell* what it is." Dissatisfied with that kind of vagueness about something so vital to humanity, Constable set out to paint light. He saw that when the light changed, a place changed. It was his earliest and most important discovery. "The world is wide," he said, "no two days are alike, not even two hours, neither were there ever two leaves of a tree alike since the creation of the world, and the genuine productions of art, like those of nature, are all distinct from each other."

He worked hard now, both to discover himself and to establish himself. He sent pictures to the Royal Academy,

THE HAY WAIN, 1821. *A farm wagon fords the River Stour on a fresh and verdant summer's day.*

Maria Bicknell, 1816

Constable's happiest years began in 1816 with his marriage to Maria Bicknell, the delicate beauty in the portrait above. Delighted with their seven children and buoyed by Maria's support, he produced his most composed and stable works: the six "canal" pictures. "Now," he wrote, "I have a kingdom of my own both fertile and populous—my landscapes and my children." The Hay Wain, at left, third in the "canal" series, won him fame and honors in Paris, but not at home.

he copied family portraits for aristocrats, he even traveled about England to paint, as landscape artists were expected to do. In the Lake District Constable met William Wordsworth and, although they were never to become friends, he found in Wordsworth's poetry a perfect statement of the "natural" values he sought for his own art. His search would, of course, be successful. As one modern critic has said, "Few painters had Constable's power to bring the infinite facts of nature into one single idea, and, with almost unconscious naturalness, to translate them into a poetic image." Wordsworth and Constable, though they had little to do with each other, were the channels through which the English Romantic movement was to express itself in its most profound terms.

But it was a lonely course Constable had set for himself. "I see him silhouetted," wrote Charles Leslie, his friend and first biographer, "coming from nowhere, going nowhere, but producing work of wonderful quality within lines sharply distinct from the ambiance of history." There have been artists and writers who have prided themselves on being "distinct from the ambiance of history," but Constable was not one of

them. From the very beginning he worked to be understood and accepted.

In 1810 Constable came of age as a revolutionary artist. He had been struggling since about 1806 to free himself from the rules governing traditional landscape painting. Fortunately for art, Constable's new "realism" was brilliantly suffused by his romantic imagination, and his work, with its broad sweeps of color and movement, reveals a man who saw poetry lying at the root of the everyday things of life. He had emerged, too, as an artist who had a keen double vision for what was happening around him. One part of him saw what most people saw when they set off to labor in the fields or factories along the River Stour; the other part of him invested these humble sights with a profound spiritual significance. It was a way of looking at life that Wordsworth described as "far more deeply informed." Constable himself was fond of quoting a couplet by the Suffolk poet George Crabbe:

It is the soul that sees; the outward eyes
Present the subject, but the mind descries.

Constable's "outward eyes" were those of a gentleman farmer, a corn

merchant, and, since the sea was so near, a sailor. They were also the eyes of a naturalist and meteorologist. He was a dreamer who constantly demanded hard facts. He crowded his sketchbooks with the facts—carts, plows, sailing tackle, notes about the weather—and then, in his paintings, made them all subservient to "nature," the wonderful and mysterious force that controlled everything.

He was fascinated by time. When work on a picture continued long past the hour or day to which it belonged, he would go to great trouble to get every detail correct. *The Cornfield* (1826) is a view of the Stour Valley on a hot July day, but it was later in the year when Constable began to work on the foreground. We find him consulting one Mr. Phillips, a botanist, and receiving this advice:

At this season all the tall grasses are in flower, bogrush, bullrush, teasel. The white bindweed now hangs its flowers over the branches of the hedge; the wild carrot and hemlock flowers in banks of hedges, cow parsley, water plantain, etc.; the heath hills are purple at this season; the rose-coloured persicaria in wet ditches is now very pretty; the catchfly graces the hedge-row, as also the ragged robin; bramble is now in flower, poppy, mallow, thistle, nop, etc.

Constable's religious attitude toward landscape, his "inner eye," was obvious even as his career began. Sometimes it overwhelmed him and made him doubt everything he was trying to do: "Nothing can exceed the beauty of the country," he wrote, "—it makes pictures seem sad trumpery, even those that possess most of nature." Sometimes it humbled him: "Remember the great were not made for me, nor I for the great. . . . My limited and abstract art is to be found under every hedge, and in every lane." When he saw the kind of landscape that was popular at the Royal Academy, he saw blasphemy: "Good God!—what a sad thing it is that this lovely art is so wrested to its own destruction—only used to blind our eyes and senses from seeing the sun shine, the fields bloom, the trees blossom, and to hear the foliage rustle—the old black, rubbed-out, dirty bits of canvas to take the place of God's own works."

The art world Constable set out to enter—rather than conquer—was dominated by members of the Royal Academy, most of them portrait painters and what were called "history" painters. The acknowledged leader of the portrait painters was Sir Thomas Lawrence, who captured the elegance of Regency England and gave his sitters the heroic attitudes that the long years of war against Napoleon had made popular. History painters turned out stories, morals, and ancedotes. Battles, national events, idealized cottage scenes, episodes from the Bible, Shakespeare, or the classical poets—these were the subjects people liked to have hanging on their walls.

The Royal Academy, which had been in existence for nearly forty years, set the standards for what was acceptable as art, serving a clientele drawn mainly from the middle class. Constable and the Academy—and its customers—were at odds from the very start. He flatly refused to be what he called "a ladies' and gentlemen's painter," and

Academy clients objected to what they called his "low" art. His brushwork offended them, and they could not understand why anyone would want pictures of ordinary barns, mills, and laborers. They wanted theatrical pictures like *Belshazzar's Feast* by John Martin, which resembled a glittering scene from one of Handel's operas. *The Blind Fiddler,* by David Wilkie, allowed them to indulge their Christian compassion for the poor, and they enjoyed huge, action-filled canvases like Benjamin West's *Battle of La Hague.* The public's eagerness for glossy miracles of technique and pictorial novelty shocked Constable. "In an age such as this," he declared, "painting should be *understood,* not looked on with blind wonder, not considered only a poetic aspiration, but as a pursuit, *legitimate, scientific* and *mechanical.*"

*F*ortunately for Constable, this period saw the foundation of another long-lasting friendship. Friendships with John Dunthorne and Sir George Beaumont had each led to remarkable extensions of his art, and now, a chance meeting with Dr. Fisher, the rector of Langham, led to the friendship that was to sustain him in the long days of rejection ahead.

The parish of Langham lay to the south of Dedham Vale, and it was on a hill not far from Langham church that Constable sat to draw his favorite view of the river scenery below. Dr. Fisher liked to make water-color sketches of the same lovely farmland. After he became bishop of Salisbury, Fisher invited Constable to visit him there. Constable was to find a scene he would make almost as famous as Flatford Mill—the tall, pale, dizzily spired cathedral rising out of the water meadows and the sluggish river, the kind of river he liked, winding over Salisbury Plain. And there, too, in 1811, he was to meet the wisest, most understanding person in his life—John Fisher, the bishop's nephew

and a newly ordained minister as well.

Constable spent these formative years not only in discovering "his path"; he was also busy doing all the things other young artists of the time did. He showed paintings of the fashionable Lake District at the Royal Academy, and he entered into the spirit of the Napoleonic Wars by going to Chatham and painting *H.M.S. Victory,* May, 1803.

At Chatham I hired a boat to see the men of war, which are there in great numbers. I sketched the *Victory* in three views. She was the flower of the flock, a three decker of (some say) 112 guns. She looked very beautiful, fresh out of dock and newly painted. When I saw her they were bending the sails.

Superb sea painter that Constable was, with an expert knowledge of shipping, he found the sea itself formless and horrifying. He never sought it out. His magnificent sea pictures were nearly all painted when chance circumstances brought him within sight of the ocean.

Although Constable was at the height of his power between the years 1810 and 1818, particularly with his *Boat-building near Flatford Mill,* painted entirely in the open air during the summer of 1815, it was not until the end of that decade that he set out to force the public to accept him as an important landscape artist. His aim was to produce for the Academy a number of very large pictures of Flatford Mill and Dedham Vale that would incorporate both his scientific view of nature and a remarkable new painting technique. The canvas size was deliberate, calculated to impress the Academy and test himself: "A large canvas will show you what you cannot do, a small one will only show you what you can do." And so we find him cheerfully writing John Fisher, "I do not consider myself at work [unless] I am before a six-foot canvas." He called this venture his "canal" pictures, and the series was undertaken during what were probably the happiest years of his life.

The basis of this happiness was his marriage to Maria Bicknell. She was the granddaughter of Dr. Rhudde, rector of East Bergholt, a fierce, rich, authoritarian old man who seems to have distrusted Constable long before the artist met Maria. The dislike was so obvious that when the two fell in love they lived in dread of the rector's finding out about their relationship and disinheriting Maria. The lovers were forced into a miserable and frustrating secrecy that Constable found particularly distressing. He was thirty-three when this secret courtship began and thirty-nine when the wise John Fisher persuaded the unhappy couple to stop worrying about Dr. Rhudde's money and get married. He performed the ceremony at Saint Martin-in-the-Fields on October 2, 1816. John Fisher himself had been married a few months earlier, to Wordsworth's niece, and now the four of them left London by coach for a honeymoon in Dorset—bringing Constable to one of his chance meetings with the sea, and to the subject of his most profound sea painting, *Weymouth Bay*.

On their return from the honeymoon, the Constables set up housekeeping in London, first in Bloomsbury, then at 35 Charlotte Street in Soho, and Constable began traveling to Suffolk to make oil sketches for pictures he later painted in his studio in town. It is these oil sketches that contain the essence of his genius. In them we see art entering a new dimension. Executed entirely for his own instruction and joy, they are masterpieces that fuse the elements of the natural scene—light, earth, and water. Other painters had sketched their first ideas in oils rather than pencil or chalk, but none like Constable. Something unique and amazing happened here. A moment of time in the open air was transposed to canvas, or to the specially prepared sheets of paper he often used. Constable once said, "If I were bound with chains I should break them, and with a single hair round me I should feel uncomfortable." In these tremendously immediate paintings, each a complete statement in itself, he found the total artistic freedom he needed.

In the six "canal" pictures of 1819 to 1825, which grew out of these sketches, Constable combined his inspired vision of landscape with, he hoped, sufficient traditional feeling to make the canvases acceptable to the public, and particularly to the artists at the Royal Academy. But his colors hadn't been blended properly, people said, and the white flecks of paint he used as highlights were dismissed as "Constable's snow."

The Hay Wain, completed in 1821, was the third canvas in the series to fail to find a buyer at the Royal Academy. It was hanging in a gallery called the British Institute when two young leaders of the French Romantic movement, Théodore Géricault and Charles Nodier, saw it and were overwhelmed.

French painting was dominated then by a facile style known as classicism, a mixture of militarism and "Grecian" sensuousness that reached its peak in the work of David (which Constable thought derived "from the brothel"). It was in 1824, when the war between official art and Romantic art filled the Salon with controversy, that a dealer named John Arrowsmith, learning of Constable from Nodier, brought *The Hay Wain* to Paris.

Constable had been reluctant to sell, although, as he said, "I need the money dreadfully." As a conservative English patriot who had lived through twenty years of war with France, he could think of the French only as enemies. He also held the Englishman's traditional view of Paris: "Think of the lovely valleys amid the peaceful farm houses of Suffolk forming a scene of exhibition to amuse the gay and frivolous Parisians!"

Amusement was hardly what *The Hay Wain* provided in Paris. Constable didn't read French, but his wife translated the news for him. He could hardly believe it. "My landscapes have made an epoch there," he wrote. "They wonder where the *brightness* comes from." The commissions rolled in, and the critics raved; two pictures, *The Hay Wain* and *A View on the Stour,* were placed on special exhibit at the Louvre, and Charles X awarded him the Salon's Gold Medal. Constable was overcome. "What a feather!" he exclaimed. It was the first official acknowledgment of his genius.

No one knows why Constable quarreled with Arrowsmith, but suddenly, just when it seemed that he might become a leader of European art, he flatly refused to let "the French man" have any more pictures. Certainly Constable disliked having to work on a commissioned basis. Commissions were "jobs" and having to do a job irritated him. Arrowsmith seems to have been neither very generous nor very tactful, and one day, with the short temper for which he was famous, Constable sent him packing.

The break with France came at an unfortunate time. A few months later Constable finished the sixth and last painting in the "canal" series: *The Leaping Horse* is his most dramatic canvas and a superb culmination to the group of paintings with which he made his bid for fame. Yet, "no one picture ever departed from my easel with more anxiety on my part," Constable declared, and his premonitions were correct: the Academy was outraged and the painting was not sold.

Nor was *The Leaping Horse* shown in Paris. Nevertheless, twenty of Constable's canvases had gone to France and there they forged a link in the chain that would result in an altogether new concept of art. Delacroix changed his palette because of them; a group of landscape painters working in the Forest of Fontainebleau was influenced by those brilliant East Anglian views, and the generation that followed the Barbizon School, as it was called, would make wonderful use of Constable's discoveries. Would the Impressionist movement have been hurried forward had Millet, Corot, and Delacroix seen *The Leaping Horse* or Constable's oil sketches? The "ifs" surrounding Constable's moment of glory in Paris have intrigued art historians ever since.

Constable was never again to know fame in his lifetime. As though even this brief success had to be tempered with disappointment, the first serious signs of

John Fisher, circa 1817

Late in life, devastated by his wife's death in 1828 and discouraged by the public indifference to his work, Constable sought solace from Archdeacon John Fisher, the steadfast friend portrayed above. "You need a staff at present," responded Fisher. "Lean on me hard." At his friend's home in Salisbury, Constable found not only encouragement but also a majestic subject for his art: Salisbury Cathedral. In the painting at right, Constable included a rainbow, suggesting perhaps that his visit with Fisher had rekindled his hopes.

SALISBURY CATHEDRAL FROM THE MEADOWS, circa 1831. *Fisher's home is to the right of the cathedral.*

Mrs. Constable's tuberculosis emerged in 1824. They went to Brighton for her health, and while she rested he painted sea pictures, including *Brighton Beach, with Colliers* and *The Marine Parade and Chain Pier, Brighton.* Indeed, it was here that he heard of the sensation his work had created in Paris.

His wife's illness, his increasingly large family (they were to have seven children by 1828), his problematic position with the Royal Academy—all contributed to a new seriousness in Constable. He worried about money. The collapse of agriculture after the Napoleonic Wars was ruining the prosperity of his beloved Stour Valley, and it was a great shock to Constable, faithful believer in the old social order, to hear that the starving villagers of East Bergholt were rioting. The financial situation was sometimes so bad that the mill, a source of income for Constable, failed to make a profit.

Now and then there were hints of fame. Constable described one of them in a letter to a friend:

In the coach yesterday coming from Suffolk, were two gentlemen and myself, all strangers to each other. In passing through the valley about Dedham, one of them remarked to me, on my saying that it was beautiful, "Yes, sir, this is *Constable's* country!"

Most important, there were the pleasures of nature: "The trees and the clouds seem to ask me to try and do something like them, and that's no small return for a life of labour." Words like "light," "dews," "breezes," "blooms," and "freshness" run through his letters and lectures, making us feel the very air of George IV's England. Everything connected with the weather fascinated Constable. "As I rode home a complete arch of rainbow came down to my very feet: I saw my dog running through it."

*A*s a miller's son, Constable was proud of having a miller's weather eye, but it was not until the publication in 1820 of a book entitled *The Climate of London* that Constable—and indeed, all the writers and painters of the Romantic movement—discovered what might be called the mete-

orological facts of life. Luke Howard, the author and the first modern weatherman, classified clouds into categories—cirrus, cumulus, and so forth—and gave a scientific basis to the atmospheric changes that painters had used for mood or simply as decoration. While Shelley was writing "The Cloud" and Goethe was writing to Luke Howard himself, praising him for discovering in meteorology "a symbol of the universal law," Constable was out "skying," recording the sky in all its moods. He worked fast, sketching on sheets of oiled paper in the lid of his paintbox, and in 1822 alone he executed more than fifty brilliant little pictures. "It will be difficult," he said, "to name a class of landscape in which the sky is not the keynote, the standard of scale, and the chief organ of sentiment. . . . The sky is the source of light in nature, and governs everything."

Having freed himself of the literary feelings that surrounded conventional landscape painting, Constable now realized that an artist did not constantly need to seek fresh scenes: the mood, form, and tones of a single landscape were in a state of everlasting change and permutation because of the effect of light. Howard's book helped him to explain things for which there had previously been no correct language, and now he was able to say in one of his lectures that landscape painting "is scientific as well as poetic; . . . imagination alone never did, and never can, produce works that are to stand by a comparison with realities."

Constable's sky sketches were made in Hampstead. In 1820, when he first went to live there, it was a large, comfortable village, only a shilling coach-ride from London. The Heath, with its ponds and gravel works, was still very wild. "Our little drawing-room commands a view unequalled in Europe," he wrote John Fisher. His favorite sketching and painting spot was near Branch Hill pond. Foggy, noisy London lay below. It was while watching the effect of the clouds from these heights that Constable formed the corollary to his ideas about light: "I live by shadows," he said. "To me shadows are realities."

Like the Stour Valley and Salisbury Plain, Hampstead Heath was to become an important personal landscape for Constable. But when his beloved wife, Maria, died in November, 1828, he chose none of these for his astonishing memorial to her.

Many years earlier, during his frustrated courtship, Constable had discovered an ancient tower overlooking the Thames estuary at Hadleigh. He had told Maria about it in a letter: "At Hadleigh there is a ruin of a castle which from its situation is a really fine place . . . ." He had never revisited the spot but now, his wife dead, he remembered it and how it had seemed to represent the futility of human endeavor. The majestic sketch that he made for the picture of this castle, which he entitled *The Nore,* is overwhelming in its grief. One critic has said that nothing equals its sense of desolation except Van Gogh's last paintings of empty fields. Although more than a century was to pass before the importance of the finished work was understood, the luminous *Hadleigh Castle* of 1829 marks one of those great and

rare advances in the history of painting.

Constable was elected a member of the Royal Academy a few months after his wife's death. It was his fourth attempt to join the Academy, and he had been accepted by a margin of a single vote. His great contemporary J. M. W. Turner came around to tell him the good news and was full of congratulations. Sir Thomas Lawrence, president of the Academy, was, however, genuinely surprised. Constable, he commented, "ought to think himself lucky." Although Constable had once remarked that "the Royal Academicians know as much about landscape as they do about the Kingdom of Heaven," the election meant a great deal to him. A man who honored institutions, he believed his acceptance by the highest art institute in the land meant people would look at his pictures with new respect. He felt vindicated at last.

Gradually the depression following his wife's death lifted. He traveled to the English places where he felt himself a "welcome guest" during these last years. "I must again repeat the necessity of keeping one's mind alive to that external nature with which we are surrounded," he said. "We exist but in a Landscape and we are the creatures of a Landscape." At Coleorton he stayed with his old friend Sir George Beaumont. The Romantic movement was now nearing its end, and Sir George, in a truly romantic gesture, had erected in his garden an ornamental cenotaph to Sir Joshua Reynolds. Constable painted this elaborate garden scene, introducing a stag that seems to link the eighteenth century with the Victorian age, now so near. It is a strange picture, almost academic in its artificial sadness and unusually finished brushwork, as if Constable were making an effort to please a sentimental public.

In 1832 he exhibited his most ambitious attempt at history painting. He had worked on *Waterloo Bridge from*

Whitehall Stairs for thirteen years, and the subject—the new bridge over the Thames being opened by the prince regent to celebrate the defeat of Napoleon—was a popular one. But the picture was not popular. Constable's wonderful description of light playing on the water and on the crowded banks was, as usual, dismissed as "spotty."

In 1835 he sold the last of his great Stour scenes, *The Valley Farm,* for three hundred pounds. He spent most of the money fitting out his son Charles for the sea. In February, 1837, he gave his last lecture at the Royal Academy school at Somerset House, and was cheered by the students. He walked home with a friend who said, "We parted at the west end of Oxford Street, laughing—I never saw him alive again." Constable died suddenly at about midnight on March 31, 1837, after a long day working on a picture called *Arundel Mill.* There was a Rubens print near his feet and Cowper's *Letters,* his favorite bedside book, near his hand. He was sixty-one years old. He was buried near the wall in Hampstead churchyard, beneath the clear skies from which he had learned the profound truths that fill his landscapes.

Nearly all his work remained in storage until 1888, when his daughter bequeathed it to the nation. Thereafter, most Englishmen would see John Constable as the perfect interpreter of their countryside; indeed, *The Hay Wain* became, as one modern critic has said, "part of the landscape of every English mind."

It is ironic that as total acceptance of Constable's vision of landscape art was beginning, the French impressionists—Cézanne, Monet, Manet—were struggling against the same kind of official hostility that Constable had encountered. But in time, they too would enjoy the public adulation that their English forebear finally earned.

Ronald Blythe was born in "Constable country," and today descendants of the artist are among his neighbors in the part of Suffolk he describes in his book Akenfield: Portrait of an English Village.

"God Almighty's Style"

SEASCAPE STUDY WITH RAIN CLOUDS, circa 1824–25, *perhaps near Brighton*

While his contemporaries wooed the English public with facile pictures of spectacular battles and sentimental moments, Constable irritated them by drawing his inspiration not from history or literature but from nature itself, and by simply painting what he saw: clouds, canals, ponds, and heaths. His intention, he announced, was to paint in "God Almighty's style." In preparing paintings for exhibit, it is true, Constable may have made concessions to popular taste—adding a hint of narrative, a touch of finish, or a nod to history. But in his oil sketches (above and on the following pages) he was a daring experimenter. Seated before his subject, his paintbox on his knees, Constable began in about 1816 to dash off rough impressions of the scenes he knew so well: Brighton Beach under changing skies, Hampstead's ponds and clouds, Weymouth Bay before a storm. In these studies, made largely for his own instruction and pleasure, Constable realized his chief ambition: "to give one brief moment caught from fleeting time a lasting and sober existence."

WEYMOUTH BAY, circa 1816

Branch Hill Pond: Evening, circa 1821–22

STUDY OF CLOUDS, 1822, *perhaps at Hampstead*

BRIGHTON BEACH, 1824

COAST SCENE, 1828, *perhaps near Brighton at evening*

Houses That Just Grew

Before the energy shortage makes our glass boxes obsolete

we might look to the yurt,

the igloo,

and the stone cottage for a lesson in efficiency

When I lived in the Berkshire Hills of western Massachusetts, some of my neighbors owned quite splendid rectilinear houses of the Bauhaus persuasion. The cynosure of all eyes, however, was a nearby hilltop farmhouse with a sagging roof, small rooms, low ceilings, a creaky staircase, windows that tilted at rakish angles, and a kitchen dominated by an enormous cast-iron stove that radiated a sense of well-being. The nearby Bauhaus boxes with their central heating were not nearly so well-armed against the New England weather, and through their inevitable picture windows one looked at nature as though it were happening on a television screen. Somehow, for all their technological advantages, none of the modern architects had even come close to the achievement of the anonymous carpenter who built that farmhouse in the 1760's with an unerring sense of what suited the landscape.

As a result of recent energy problems, much of modern architecture has begun to seem as out of place in its way as those Bauhaus houses did in theirs. The typical office building, for example, far from being one of the great achievements of twentieth-century technology, has been revealed as a monster of inefficiency. Studies show that many such buildings lose half their coolness in the summer and half their heat in the winter. Engineers estimate, furthermore, that with certain design changes it would be possible to cut energy consumption in many buildings by 40 per cent, since much of the power goes into duplicating on the inside what nature is already providing on the outside. In and around New York City, the architect and energy consultant Richard G. Stein points out, the outside temperature is entirely suitable for introduction into a building during some five hundred hours a year, a full sixth of the time the building is occupied.

The trouble is cumulative. We are burning up everything at a great rate to protect ourselves from an environment that has become increasingly hostile because we have been burning up everything at such a great rate. We must ask, Stein says, whether the increase in energy per capita has resulted in a comparable increase in the quality of life per capita. In most cases, he says, the answer is no.

Do things have to be this way? For a clue to our answer, we need look no further than our eighteenth-century farmhouse. In the language of the architecture schools, such a structure represents "vernacular architecture"—i.e., the houses, igloos, yurts, and kampongs that people without architects have traditionally built with palm fronds, fieldstones, mud and wattle, or whatever else they had at hand. The study of vernacular architecture has suddenly become of vital interest, for there are lessons to be learned from the way folk architects, often working in difficult environments and with acutely limited resources, have solved problems of shelter.

The Bedouin tent, for example, turns out on closer examination to be a beautifully refined tensile structure of the sort Buckminster Fuller likes to design —a portable home that answers the nomad herder's need for mobility and is eminently adaptable to desert conditions. It can be dismantled, rolled up, and loaded on a camel in less than an hour. In a climate of extreme temperature fluctuations, it furnishes shelter, shade, warmth, or cooling drafts of air as required. Today the tents are fast disappearing as the nomad population diminishes, and most of the ones I have seen in the Sahara were rather motheaten; nevertheless, before the arrival of the oil well and the Land Rover, the architectural technology of the Bedouins was a perfect illustration of what Fuller calls a "dymaxion" system—one that makes maximum use of minimum energy. Long ago, in fact, its beauty and utility excited the admiration of men like Sir Richard Burton and Charles Doughty, two of the first Europeans to live among the Bedouins. Doughty goes into loving detail in his classic nineteenth-century account, *Travels in Arabia Deserta*:

The Aarab tent, which they call the *beyt* (pl. *byût*) *es-shaar,* "abode, booth or house of hair," that is of black worsted or hair-cloth, has, with its pent roof, somewhat the form of a cottage. The tent-stuff, strong and rude, is defended by a list sewed under at the heads of the am'dan, and may last out, they say, a generation, only wearing thinner. . . . The Arabian tent strains strongly upon all the staves, and in good holding-ground, may resist the boisterous blasts which happen at the crises of the year, especially in some deep mountainous valleys. Even in weak sand the tents are seldom overblown. . . . The tent-stuff is seamed of narrow lengths of the housewives' rude worsted weaving; the yarn is their own spinning, of the mingled wool of the sheep and camels' and goats' hair together. Thus it is that the cloth is blackish: we read in the Hebrew Scripture, "Black as the tents of Kedar." . . .

When the tent-cloth is stretched upon the stakes, to this roof they hang the tent-curtains, often one long skirt-cloth which becomes the walling of the nomad booth: the selvedges are broached together with wooden skewers. The booth front is commonly left open, to the half at least we have seen, for the *mukaad* or men's sitting room; the other which is the women's and household side, is sometimes seen closed (when they would not be espied, whether sleeping or cooking) with a fore-cloth; the women's part is always separated from the men's apartment by a hanging, commonly not much more than breast or neck high, at the waist-poles of the tent. . . . In winter they sometimes load the back-cloth ground-hem with great stones, and fence their open front at the men's side with dry bushes. The tent side-cloths can be shifted according to the wind and sun: thus the back of the . . . booth may become in a moment the new front.

If we want our young architects to learn how to work more closely with the sun and the elements, instead of constantly trying to subdue them, we should send them out among the troglodytes and the lake dwellers and into the jungles and marshes of the world. Many of the solutions to be found there come startlingly close to the wildest dreams of the West's avant-garde designers. An Eskimo igloo, for instance, anticipates William Katavolos's vision of structures that materialize when they are needed and vanish when they are not. It can be erected almost as rapidly as a Bedouin tent, even in a snowstorm: two Eskimos, working only with knives for sawing out blocks of snow, can build one in about an hour. With the door sealed and a blubber lamp burning, the temperature inside soon reaches 65 degrees, though the outside temperature may drop to 20 or 30 degrees below zero. Aesthetically, as an example of form following function, the igloo can hardly be faulted. "One of the most chaste pieces of architecture I ever saw," wrote Charles Francis Hill, an early Arctic explorer.

From a technological point of view, the igloo is a triumph of thermal engineering. "The igloo dome is constructed of a sloping spiral of snow blocks," explains *Architectural Forum*:

It becomes stronger and more windproof by a glaze of ice that forms on the interior because of body heat and an oil lamp. This ice is also a radiant heat reflector, like foil on insulation, and is a smooth and durable floor covering. The dome offers maximum resistance to winter winds and exposes the minimum surface to their chilling effect. It encloses the largest volume with the least material and forms a shape that has no cold spots in relation to a . . . source of heat.

Finally, since the igloo melts every spring, it is the world's first self-demolishing house—a feature whose value we now (after Levittown and the Sears Tower) begin to appreciate.

With much the same economy of means, the Ma'dan, or "Marsh Arabs," who live at the mouths of the Tigris and Euphrates, build the airiest of homes with the only material available to them in abundance—the giant swamp reed *Phragmites communis*, which grows twenty feet high. Massive bundles of these reeds, tied together with reed twine, are set into the ground eighteen to twenty feet apart. Then the ends are bent over and joined together to form a parabolic arch. A series of these arches, set at four-foot intervals, forms the ribs of a sturdy barrel vault, which is cross-braced with other reed bundles and covered with overlapping layers of split-reed matting; the matting at the sides can be opened or closed as wind and weather dictate. Wilfred Thesiger, who spent several years among the Ma'dan,

reports that the largest of these structures—the *mudhifs*, or guest houses—are 20 feet wide and 120 feet long.

The Ma'dan houses, which make such an elegant virtue of necessity, blend beautifully with the marshes. Folk architects are invariably masters at harmonizing their work with the environment. (It appears that the architects of the Industrial Age are the only systematic ravishers of landscapes.) This harmony is nowhere more impressive than in the jungles of Equatorial Africa, where villages are traditionally interlaced among the trees and distributed with such style and ingenuity as to present town planners with a model of ecological integration. This was one of the aspects of Equatorial Africa that fascinated some of the early European explorers. "Indeed, what most strikes the traveller in coming from the sea-coast to this inland country, is the large size, neatness and beauty of the villages," wrote Paul du Chaillu, the zoologist and explorer who in the 1850's and 1860's conducted the first serious studies of gorilla life. In a typical equatorial village, he noted in his journal, "several houses are connected so as to form a square, with a common yard or garden in the middle, in which grow magnificent palm-trees. Behind the houses, too, are very frequently groups of plantain and lime trees. The village being thus composed of a series of small quadrangles and back-gardens containing trees with beautiful foliage, the whole effect is very charming."

In western Rajasthan, at the edge of the Great Indian Desert, where I am writing this, the farming tribes build equally organic villages that rise out of the terrain like circular clumps of mushrooms. Around the central unit, the family compound, are small, specialized structures—sleeping quarters, a kitchen, a food-storage unit, and, for the animals' food, a granary. As in Sahara architecture, the adobe walls of Rajasthani houses are thick enough to absorb the sun slowly during the day and then re-radiate the heat after sundown, when the temperature suddenly drops 30 or 40

degrees. The roofs are made of thick thatch laid over an umbrella of branches, and the floors consist of packed cow dung worn smooth by bare feet.

It is a noble and versatile material, this cow dung, as I had reason to learn the week I arrived. Having rented an empty house, I asked the landlord's English-speaking daughter whether she had any fresh sheets for me. She said something about having to wait until the next day because it wouldn't dry—which I assumed to mean she'd have to wash some first. But the next morning, to my utter astonishment, she showed up with her mother, carrying bowls of fresh cow dung—i.e., "sheet"—which they softened still further with water and then spread with a whiskbroom over the old cement-hard floors. (I hadn't realized until then that they, too, were of dung.) After drying all day, the dung had a beautifully handmade look and covered the floors with a khaki-colored layer, rather like a fiber rug—cool, clean, and resilient. In a well-run household, apparently, the floor is redunged in this fashion every three weeks or so, not only for appearance's sake, but because a fresh layer of cow dung is said to discourage insects.

Our Western tradition of vernacular architecture has, of course, come up with quite different solutions to quite different problems. But even in the harsh European climates, where stone houses serve as fortresses against the winter, people never neglected the movements of the sun the way contemporary glass-box architects do. On the contrary, the European folk tradition calls for taking advantage of whatever sun happens to be available. Sixty years ago John Synge was surprised to find that the people of the Aran Islands, off the coast of Galway, still responded to the sun and the wind in almost aboriginal ways. In his book *The Aran Islands* he noted that even the islanders' knowledge of time depended, in a roundabout sort of way, on the direction of the wind:

Nearly all the cottages are built . . . with two doors opposite each other, the more sheltered of which lies open all day to give light to the interior. If the wind is northerly the south door is opened, and the shadow of the door-post moving across the kitchen floor indicates the hour; as soon, however, as the wind changes to the south the other door is opened, and the people, who never think of putting up a primitive dial, are at a loss.

This system of doorways has another curious result. It usually happens that all the doors on one side of the village pathway are lying open with women sitting about on the thresholds, while on the other side the doors are shut and there is no sign of life. The moment the wind changes everything is reversed, and sometimes when I come back to the village after an hour's walk there seems to have been a general flight from one side of the way to the other. In my own cottage the change of doors alters the whole tone of the kitchen, turning it from a brilliantly-lighted room looking out on a yard and laneway to a sombre cell with a superb view of the sea.

Primitive architecture, in other words, has less to do with "the play . . . of forms under light," as Le Corbusier conceived of his métier, than with the work of man in nature: it is the physical expression of a particular approach to life. The Aran islander, like the Rajasthani peasant or the equatorial African, knew how to satisfy his architectural needs without doing violence to his surroundings; his house was a bridge between himself and the environment. Twentieth-century architecture, with a few notable exceptions, has utterly failed to arrive at a similar entente with nature; its principal effect has been to accelerate the process of depersonalization. I do not know (and fear to ask) what inroads it may have made in the Aran Islands since Synge was there, but I am prepared to testify in painful detail about its depredations on the northern coast of Majorca, once one of the most beautiful islands in the Mediterranean.

For centuries the villages and isolated farms scattered along this mountainous coast were built by ordinary peasants and fishermen employing vernacular forms and techniques, including elements that could be traced back to Roman, Moorish, and medieval origins

In the compound in rural Togo, above, individual thatched houses, snug even during the six-month rainy season, are provided for each wife and child. Others serve as granaries and kitchens. The tent below, made of hand-woven goat hair, shelters a Bedouin family in Algeria. Airy and cool, it is easily dismantled for transportation by camel to new grazing grounds.

With the help of neighbors, a family in western Rajasthan built the complex of mud huts above. The roof thatch is easily replaced; fresh layers of cow dung renew the floors. The design of the large house below, located in Iraq, has not changed in six thousand years. Made of twenty-foot-tall local reeds, it faces Mecca and has a fine view of the lower Tigris.

and that had been handed down from father to son. They worked without anything so sophisticated as a plumb line, but with patience, energy, and some clearly conceived ideas of the useful and the beautiful. Frank Lloyd Wright would have loved these houses for the way they are rooted in the ground, leaning against each other in the villages or rising out of the terraced olive orchards of the farms along the coast. Often they sit at the edge of a cliff, firmly anchored to an outcropping of bedrock. Their walls are thick, consisting of a double layer of massive fieldstones. Before the advent of Portland cement, the spaces between the stones were plastered up with a mortar made of earth and lime. This mortar matches the golden coloring of the stone and seems to breathe with the wall, growing more beautiful with age: I have seen walls a hundred and fifty years old that still do not require repointing. The recipe for this mortar, incidentally, is said to date from the *tiempo de los moros,* the time of the Moors (who were expelled in A.D. 1229), and in former days the masons used to mix a great batch of it and leave it to cure for seven months, turning it over with each new moon.

The windows are small and there are not many of them, but they are fitted with *persianas*—i.e., "Persian" louvered shutters—which provide privacy and shade while allowing the air to circulate freely when it is hot. In their heating and cooling action, these are typical Mediterranean houses, for though the walls look immutably static, their thermal effects are eminently dynamic, keeping the interior cool in the summer and retaining its fireplace warmth in the winter. As Richard Stein explains, "The mass of the heavy masonry construction achieves a delicate balance with the daily heat flow. It continues to pick up heat during the day, but the heat just begins to penetrate into the space at nightfall. It continues to lose heat to the inside space during the cool night and is then ready to begin its diurnal cycle again."

The old Majorcan houses have hand-hewn roof beams of local poplar, impervious to termites and almost indestructible. Across them goes a layer of fresh-cut cane, laced tightly together with hemp to support a roof of heavy Spanish tiles—the old hand-made ones fashioned from a slab of terra cotta bent over the maker's knee. Inside, the ceilings are low, the walls not quite parallel or perpendicular but covered with snowdrifts of whitewash, the product of generations of weekly whitewashings, so that not one corner remains unrounded. The rooms convey a great sense of security, not only because the walls are so solid but because the effect is that of a cave, or, as the environmentalist Wade Greene once said, "a womb with a view."

During the past twenty years, however, on the assumption that a wall is a wall and the cheaper the better, people have stopped building with fieldstone. The favorite material now is cement block; contractors claim that it "takes too long" and hence costs too much to build in stone. Yet the economics of cement blocks have never been proved to my satisfaction, or to that of my friend Jaime Punta ("Jim Stone-Chisel"). Jaime builds fieldstone walls nearly as fast as other men lay blocks, and his walls don't need a coat of stucco afterward. At fifty-four, he is a master in the art of building house walls and dry-wall terraces, known as *bancals;* his profession, he says rather wistfully, is that of *bancalero* rather than *banquero* (banker). When he sets about building a wall, he first lays out twenty or thirty stones in a semicircle, with himself prominently at the center. He begins at ground level by prying the heaviest boulders into place with his giant crowbar, and then continues with more manageable sizes, though there are never any easy stones to build with—they come in all sorts of irregular shapes, rarely displaying so much as a single smooth surface. But Jaime's sense of spatial relationships is almost uncanny. He picks up a stone, seemingly at random, juggles it briefly in his hands, gives it a thoughtful tap or two with his twelve-pound hammer to knock off a recalci-

trant point or bulge, and then maneuvers it neatly into its place on the wall. It always fits precisely, and never requires cement to hold it in place. One day, after watching him perform this trick for the hundredth time, I interrupted him to ask, "Jaime, how is it that you always manage to find exactly the right stone for the next space?" He laughed and shook his head. I hadn't understood. "I'm not picking out a stone for the next space," he said. "I'm making a bed for the next stone."

Nowadays, though Jaime still builds terraces and garden walls, nobody hires him to build stone houses; people have got out of the habit. The contractors say you can do the same thing in cement blocks that you can do in stone, but they're lying through their teeth. A cement block house goes up anywhere at all, with no particular reference to the lay of the land. The walls are parallel, the edges sharp, the windows too large and mechanical, and the roof, if not flat, wears dowdy orange tiles made by the same factory as the cement block. Painted in pastel shades, including baby pink, such houses bring a frivolous pistachio flavor to an ancient and dignified coast. Many of them are already incipient eyesores, and the local stone-house people refer to them contemptuously as *casas de cartón* (cardboard houses). Their picture windows and flimsy walls make them hot in the summer, cold and damp in the winter. Even nature refuses to co-operate with the cement-block houses; for some reason nothing seems to thrive in their gardens, and ten years after they have been built they look like the bulldozers just left.

There is another vital difference between the Majorcan houses of the vernacular and those of the *cartón* epoch. The old houses were built by people for themselves, by a man and his brother, and perhaps a cousin or two. They took the stones from the mountainsides; the beams were hewn from local timber. They added to their houses as they needed more space—and when they had time to spare. The average modern

householder spends twenty or thirty years paying off the mortgage on his house, but has little or nothing to say about the architectural decisions that will affect his life during that time. For the folk builder, on the other hand, with his family helpers, it was a matter not of years but of several months of effort. In Majorca it meant one summer's work for the builder and his family, each contributing as much time as he could spare from his normal occupation. The women stripped the cane for the roof, did the whitewashing, and prepared the steaming platters of rice and calamares that kept the work crew in high spirits.

In Rajasthan, where smaller structures are the rule, it takes only about three months for a man and his neighbors to build a mushroom compound so that his son can take a wife. I have seen them at it, and there is always an air of great festivity as they pat the walls into place or thatch the roof with bundles of straw. Synge noted the same party spirit in the Aran Islands, when the neighbors arrived at dawn to thatch a roof:

Like all work that is done in common on the island, the thatching is regarded as a sort of festival. From the moment a roof is taken in hand there is a whirl of laughter and talk till it is ended, and, as the man whose house is being covered is a host instead of an employer, he lays himself out to please the men who work with him.

Perhaps it is this form of energy conservation that we should try hardest to relearn from the folk builders, along with the principles of working with the sun. If, as Lewis Mumford recently told an M.I.T. audience, the "dark age is already here, only we don't know it," then these "archaic" solutions may have more relevance than we suspect. There is a certain vital relationship between the building and the inhabitant that we need to resurrect if we are going to have a modern renaissance of architecture. It may mean leaving less to the specialists and doing more for ourselves. It seems that what the tentmakers and roof thatchers have been trying to tell us, in their vernacular, is that architecture is too important to be left only to architects.

Kamante Gatura in the 1960's behind Karen House

Out of Africa, Something New

An old Kenyan remembers a
greathearted woman
who was also—as Isak Dinesen
—one of the most
gifted storytellers of all time

THE DOG AND HIS SHADOW

HE THAT WANTS ANOTHER MAN'S GOOD OFTEN LOSSES HIS OWN.

In time past was a dog returning to his village
a long a river, and he held in his mouth
large slices of meat. As he passed by
a place near river water he saw reflections
of hanging down meat in a dog's mouth —

— thinking
it was another
slice of meat,
he opened his mouth to grab it.
Down fell his meal into the current.

Kamante's rendering of an ancient tale

"I, Kamande Gatura, was cooker in her house." So begins the "back history" of the Kikuyu elder above, as dictated in his native language and translated and written out by his sons. (Their handiwork, with drawings by his father, can be seen in the fable at left, one of several appended to the old man's testament.) In his memoir, Kamande—or Kamante: the spelling depends on the transcriber—recalls his youth, half a century ago and more, when his East African homeland, Kenya, was still mostly wild, and a British colony. What makes his account particularly interesting is the fresh view he provides of his employer, opposite, the incomparable teller of tales Karen Blixen, better known to readers around the world as Isak Dinesen. When Kamante first knew her, the future author of Seven Gothic Tales, Winter's Tales, and Out of Africa was not yet an established writer, though some of her early stories had been published years before in her native Denmark. Rather, she and her Swedish husband (and second cousin), Baron Bror Blixen-Finecke, were struggling to make a success of a coffee plantation in the hills near Nairobi to which they had come in 1914. In Out of Africa she was to describe Kamante, then about nine, as she first saw him: "He was the most pitiful object that you could set eyes on. His head was big and his body terribly small and thin, the elbows and knees stood out like knots on a stick and both his legs were covered with deep running sores. . . ." She washed his legs and took him to a hospital, where he was slowly cured. Kamante never forgot "the goodness of Mrs. Karen." His memoirs, along with his drawings and photographs from the Dinesens' family album, some of which appear here and on the following pages, have been gathered by photographer Peter Beard and will be published this spring by Harcourt Brace Jovanovich under the title Longing for Darkness—an event that confirms the Greek saying, cited by Pliny the Elder, that "There is always something new out of Africa."   —O. de K., Jr.

Karen Blixen—later Isak Dinesen—on safari in Kenya

Karen Blixen in her drawing room

HOW MR DINJA-HATERN SEES ALL

KAREN HOUSE 1931

Karen House, an aerial view

"Coffee-growing is a Long Job"

"This house of Mrs. Karen rang joy day and night. Nobody felt sad. . . . She was of such good nature." Such, according to Kamante, was the prevailing atmosphere at the main building, left, of Karen Coffee, as the plantation was informally called. (The "Mr. Pinja-Hatern" at lower left is an African attempt at the name of the pilot from whose plane the photograph was taken.) In *Out of Africa*, Karen Blixen recalls the difficulty of making a living at Karen Coffee: "The land was in itself a little too high for coffee, and it was hard work to keep it going; we were never rich on the farm. But a coffee-plantation is a thing that gets hold of you and does not let you go. . . . Coffee-growing is a long job. . . . It is four or five years till the trees come into bearing, and in the meantime you will get drought on the land, or diseases, and the bold native weeds will grow up thick in the fields. . . ." The "long job" only ended—for a time—when the sacks of beans were hauled by oxen to Nairobi, below, to be taken by train to Mombasa for shipment to London. Karen Blixen found Nairobi "a motley place," but "a live place" as well. "Nairobi said to you: 'Make the most of me and of time. . . .' Generally I and Nairobi were in very good understanding, and at one time I drove through the town and thought: There is no world without Nairobi's streets."

A street in Kenya's capital, Nairobi, in the 1920's

Karen Blixen with her staff, minus Kamante

KAMANTE GATURA

"A Magnificent Enlargement"

The population of Karen Coffee was heterogeneous, taking in members of several of Kenya's tribes (Kikuyu, Luo, Wakamba, Meru, Embu), Somalis from the Horn of Africa, and a few Indians. It was, moreover, constantly being augmented. Kamante explains why: "Karen Blixen was so much liked by all people in Karen. For she was kind to anybody who was working on other farms. That means if somebody was chased away by his master she would employ him in her garden and give him places to build his house, together with a piece of land where he could grow some crops. Many people used to come from Majeng, Nairobi, even from Uganda and from Mombasa to stay. She would not expel those who were staying in her farm without working. She only liked them. . . . She was indeed an excellent woman, because she never hated anybody or any doctrine, even Mohammedans." (Kamante, at left in a photograph taken by Karen Blixen's brother, Thomas Dinesen, had been converted to Christianity by the Scotch missionaries who cured his infected leg.) In addition to Kamante (who is also visible at right, holding the dogs), two other Africans who loom large in Karen Blixen's writings are her overseer, the Somali Farah Aden, second from left in the front row in the picture directly above, and Paramount Chief Kinanjui, smoking a cigar at far right, below. "The discovery of the dark races," she wrote, "was to me a magnificent enlargement of all my world."

Kamante in about 1915

Kamante, left, and friends at workers' huts

Kikuyu dancing, perhaps at a tribal ritual or ngoma

Kamante's wife, left, and friends

Chief Kinanjui comes to call

Giraffes, with a caption by an admirer

Creatures of An Enchanted Land

"One day on her way to Nairobi, [Karen Blixen] stopped for children. They did shield a young bush buck! She gave them shillings to guard it for her returning. . . . At four o'clock she came and parked the car by the store. She told me that she had come with *Lulu*. I looked. It was a bush buck baby." In those words Kamante tells the story—which Karen Blixen herself tells in *Out of Africa*—of how the little antelope at left came to the farm. Some months after its arrival, Kamante noticed that Lulu "had preginance" and soon Lulu's baby was yet another welcome guest at Karen Coffee. All of Kenya's magnificently varied wildlife—giraffes, zebras, buffalo, eland, gazelles, monkeys, lions, rhinoceros, and elephants—brought Karen Blixen great joy. But she remained very much attached, too, to tame creatures, particularly dogs, her favorite being a Scotch deerhound, Dusk, that she received as a wedding present. (Dusk, nuzzling his mistress, opposite, looks more sinister in Kamante's drawing at left.) "The Scotch Deerhound went well with African scenery and the African Native," Karen Blixen wrote. "It may be due to the altitude, —the highland melody in all three,—for he did not look so harmonious at Sea-level. . . ."

Karen Blixen feeds the baby bushbuck, Lulu

The Scotch deerhound, Dusk, as seen by Kamante

Karen Blixen and the real Dusk

Denys Finch-Hatton and his plane

Bror Blixen with his fresh kill, a bushbuck

Bror Blixen, as seen by Kamante

An End and a Beginning

Like the fortunes of her farm, which fluctuated with the world price of coffee, Karen Blixen's emotional life had ups and downs. Her marriage, into which she had entered, it seems, at the prompting of her head rather than her heart, was a failure; while Bror Blixen (at center left with a bushbuck he had killed, and at lower left in a drawing by Kamante) was a fine hunter, he was, unhappily, no match for a woman of her intelligence, sensitivity, and character. It is, perhaps, significant that in the text, not shown here, that accompanies his drawing, Kamante identifies him not by his name but as "Mr. Barance [Baroness] Breakson husband of Mrs. Karen." In 1921 the couple was divorced. (Karen Blixen never again hunted for sport.) By then, she had formed a close friendship with an English aristocrat, Denys Finch-Hatton (the "Mr. Pinja-Hatern" of the inscription on page 104), above at the propeller of his plane, who encouraged her development as a writer. In 1931—surely the worst year of her life—her friend crashed to his death and her farm failed. After seventeen years in her beloved Africa, she had to go home to Denmark and her mother (opposite, with her on a visit). She had lost almost everything she loved, she was in poor health, she felt defeated; yet her greatest triumphs lay ahead.

Karen Blixen with her mother and two friends

Waiting for the End

The sirens screamed, the buzz bombs roared, and the indomitable Sitwells read on... and on

If it had not been for the flying bombs there would have been nothing very dramatic about that London evening in October, 1944, when I heard the three Sitwells give a reading of their poetry at the Churchill Club in Dean's Yard, Westminster.

Early in the war the club had been founded with the meliorist intent of providing social and cultural ties between the Dominion forces and the mother country. Lunch was served daily in cafeteria style, but it was better than most lunches then to be found in London. In the afternoon there was a tea—less popular than lunch—and in the evening an occasional not-too-well-attended lecture. The appearance of the Sitwells, however, promised to bring out a record crowd.

During the four months I was in London, two or three flying bombs would land daily, preceded by the wail of sirens. Five minutes later, one would hear the uneven sound of the unmanned plane's engine, rather like a badly tuned motorcycle. When this rasping sound abruptly stopped, it meant the flying bomb was going into its dive. One waited a few seconds more for the crunching explosion.

The flying bombs never bothered me very much. Each one killed about a dozen people; London had a population of eight or nine million. The odds, I felt, were in my favor. At least I felt so until the night I heard the Sitwells.

It was one of those damply mild autumn evenings that suggest spring. A little late, I hurried up the elegant staircase to slip into a folding seat at the back of a low room. The Sitwells were already on the platform. There they sat with their ancestral aplomb, the formidable trio who, in "a series of skirmishes and hand-to-hand battles against the Philistine" during the interlude between the two wars, had fired off volleys of articles, poems, and books, shouting their oddly occasional verses through megaphones, playfully changing their recreations in subsequent editions of *Who's Who* from "regretting the Bourbons" and "pied-piping" to "nitwit baiting," "not receiving or answering unnecessary correspondence," and—ominously —"waiting for the end."

Sacheverell led off that evening, a somewhat awkward figure, mumbling through a series of unintelligible verses. As an admirer of his book *Southern Baroque Art*, I found him disappointing. I should have considered this actually most normal member of the family a misfit if I had passed him on the street. Osbert, who followed him, seemed more conventionally urbane, with a long-nosed hauteur that gave him a vague resemblance to the Mad Hatter. After several references to "my brother" and "my sister," he read his "Three Nocturns," pleasant enough verse, but *fin de siècle,* almost Wildean.

Then Edith took over. I had heard her described as Tudor—but this evening, with her long face and hooded hawk eyes, she seemed massively timeless, more a portrait

The trio who "invaded the world of letters with a flourish": Sacheverell, Edith, and Osbert Sitwell, photographed by Cecil Beaton.

than a person, stylized and at the same time so bent as to appear almost hunchbacked. She wore a black robe with billowing leg-of-mutton sleeves; it might have been either a coat or a dress. A slash of lipstick accentuated the portrait quality of her face, and the nails on her spectral fingers were a gruesome red. Just as she stood up, and with a flash of innumerable rings opened a volume of her poems, the sirens sounded.

She began with what is perhaps her most noble poem, "Still Falls the Rain," written under the emotional impact of the 1940 air raids and the influence of her own developing Christian convictions.

Still falls the Rain—
Dark as the world of man, black as our loss—
Blind as the nineteen hundred and forty nails
Upon the Cross. . . .

Above her voice, above the sirens, we could now hear the stuttering reverberation of a

distant flying bomb. It was a sound we had all been hardened to. No one stirred. Edith continued in her resonant yet restrained voice, her brothers seated motionless on either side of her, Sacheverell staring into space, Osbert with his legs crossed.

Still falls the Rain
In the Field of Blood where the small
    hopes breed and the human brain
Nurtures its greed, that worm with the
    brow of Cain. . . .

The reverberation was becoming a roar. Some of the audience were growing uneasy. Not the Sitwells. Edith's voice changed in neither pitch nor tone; she neither hurried nor slowed down. The words themselves were like rain.

The wounds of the baited bear,—
The blind and weeping bear
    whom the keepers beat
On his helpless flesh . . .
    the tears of the hunted hare.
Still falls the Rain. . .

Now the roar had all but drowned out her voice. Air raid wardens on the roof had begun to blow their whistles. That meant a direct hit was imminent. People were getting down on the floor, trying to shield their heads with chairs. Edith kept on reading without the slightest change of voice or expression. No one was listening to her. No one could.

The flying bomb must have all but skimmed the roof. Then the roar of its motor began to fade as it headed across the Thames. Some seconds later there was a dullish boom, all the windows rattled and several of them cracked. Edith read on until the end, immutable.

Then sounds the voice of One who like the
    heart of man
Was once a child who among beasts has lain—
"Still do I love, still shed my innocent light,
    my Blood, for thee."

Then, barely perceptibly, she winked at us.

Francis Russell specializes in both American history and twentieth-century literary figures.

By FRANCIS RUSSELL